Concepts in social administration

Students and Ex

DATE DUE

-9 OCT 85 0

-9 F

Concepts in social administration
A framework for analysis

Anthony Forder

Routledge & Kegan Paul
London and Boston

First published in 1974
by Routledge & Kegan Paul Ltd
Broadway House, 68–74 Carter Lane,
London EC4V 5EL and
9 Park Street,
Boston, Mass. 02108, USA
Set in Linotype Pilgrim
and printed in Great Britain by
Clarke, Doble & Brendon Ltd, Plymouth
© Anthony Forder 1974

ISBN 0 7100 7869 2 (c)
      0 7100 7870 6 (p)
Library of Congress Catalog Card No. 74–75853

Ad Maiorem Dei Gloriam

Contents

Preface

Teachers of social administration in Britain are seeking a framework for the subject which transcends the study of individual services on which most of the literature is based. This problem is intensified by the fact that the provision of social services, like other forms of human behaviour, can only be fully comprehended by calling on a wide range of theoretical disciplines. These include history, geography, economics, psychology, sociology and philosophy. No single person can be a master of all these, yet elements of each are needed to understand the social services.

This book aims to contribute to this search for a framework by examining a number of concepts which seem basic to the study of the social services individually and as a whole. The selection of concepts is related to a view of the social services as institutions of a 'democratic-welfare-capitalist' state. Within this state the social services aim to give increased priority to need as the basis for the distribution of resources. They also have effects on the distribution of power, which are secondary to this central aim, but have a considerable effect on the way in which it is achieved. It is this view of the social services that gives whatever unity there is to the book's examination of somewhat disparate concepts. It does not, however, deal with those major areas of social policy that are not directly concerned with the social services. Neither does it discuss wider issues of power that ultimately determine the role of the social services in our society.

It is hoped that the book will be found particularly useful by teachers of social administration in reinforcing their students' view of the social services as a whole. It assumes some preliminary knowledge of the social services, so it may be more useful to second year than to first year students. The notes which often refer to secondary sources to which students may find readier access than to primary sources, will help them to pursue gaps in their theoretical and practical knowledge. Later chapters build on concepts discussed in earlier chapters but not to such an extent that chapters and sections cannot be taken out of order according to the interests of the reader. It is hoped that students will not be put off by difficult chapters and sections from persevering with later material. Each chapter begins with a summary of the argument to help them get a better overall view of the matters being discussed.

My thanks are due to many people who have commented on different sections of the book and encouraged me to continue. I am particularly grateful to Grace Shrouder for her comments on the earlier chapters and to Gary Littlejohn and Fred Cook for assistance in working out the material in the chapters on professionalism; also to Maureen Mulligan who has assiduously striven to turn a confused and illegible manuscript into a presentable typescript.

Chapter 1
Welfare capitalism and the social services

Summary of the argument

The term 'Welfare State' is an inadequate description of our society. It puts undue emphasis on one particular aspect of that society which distinguishes it from British society in the nineteenth century. In fact our society attempts to combine three systems based on different principles; a capitalist system based on the economic market, a democratic political system, and a welfare system.

The capitalist market economy which dominated the organisation of society in the nineteenth century has important advantages as a system for distributing resources and delegating decision-making powers. It has certain serious disadvantages, which the democratic and welfare systems, particularly the latter, are intended to counteract. However, the systems are based on different value principles which to some extent are in conflict.

Social administration is concerned with the study of the welfare system, and particularly the government-sponsored social services. It is therefore concerned with the problems of relating needs and resources in contrast to the capitalist market economy which relates supply with demand that is backed by monetary resources. By examining in subsequent chapters the implications of certain concepts it is hoped to throw light on some fundamental problems in the social services that affect the distribution of resources and the distribution of power.

'The Welfare State'

It is perhaps natural that when change occurs in any situation attention should be focused on what is new rather than on what remains unchanged. So the acceptance of the term 'the

Welfare State' to describe post-war British society reflects the
new emphasis on state responsibility for social welfare and
ignores the elements of social organisation that show continuity with the past. Penelope Hall epitomised this approach
when she wrote:[1]

> The distinguishing characteristic of the Welfare State is
> the assumption by the community, acting through the
> State, of the responsibility for providing the means
> whereby all its members can reach minimum standards
> of health, economic security and civilised living, and can
> share according to their capacity in its social and cultural
> heritage.

Slack[2] has examined a number of approaches to the definition
and assessment of 'the Welfare State', and most of these follow
the same pattern, taking the nineteenth century as the point
of reference and concentrating on differences. By some, and
particularly by its supporters, the Welfare State is seen as the
culmination of a long process to right the errors and injustices
of nineteenth-century *laissez-faire* capitalism. To others it is
an attempt to modify 'the normal play of economic forces in
a market economy',[3] a phrase which implies an acceptance
of the nineteenth-century concept of economic forces whose
operation is somehow 'more normal' if it takes place independently of human, and, in particular, government decisions about
social objectives.

Piet Thoënes[4] puts this into perspective by defining the
Welfare State as 'a form of society characterised by a system
of democratic government sponsored welfare, placed on a new
footing and offering a guarantee of collective social care to its
citizens, concurrently with the maintenance of a capitalist
system of production'. This definition includes aspects of our
social system which show continuity as well as contrast with
the nineteenth century, notably democratic control and capitalism. Thoënes still accepts the term the Welfare State, but
the definition suggests that 'welfare capitalism' might be a
more accurate designation for this form of society, or even,
if it was not so cumbrous, 'democratic welfare capitalism', as
Marshall has suggested.[5]

As Thoënes points out, this approach makes possible a

2

broader comparison with other forms of society such as feudalism or socialism, as well as the 'liberal' society of the nineteenth century. *Laissez-faire* capitalism with its reluctance to accept government responsibility for maintaining the social fabric of the state can then be seen not as a norm, but as an extreme view of the role of government which must itself be accounted for.

Capitalism and the role of money

While the roots of the capitalist ethic of nineteenth-century Britain are complex,[6] one fact is clear. It was of considerable importance at that time to the new middle-class entrepreneurs that they should be able to engage in commerce and manufacture untrammelled by government control or social obligations. On the one hand they needed freedom to introduce new methods of manufacture, and the freedom of trade to exploit the advantages that these new methods gave them. On the other hand they wanted to be able to treat labour like any other factor of production, both in moulding their employees into a tractable labour force and in exploiting a buyers' market, without having to concern themselves with the welfare of that labour force. To justify their position British entrepreneurs seized on those aspects of the classical economic model derived from the work of Adam Smith which gave them support.[7]

At the centre of the classical economic theories were certain valid propositions about the role of money and a competitive market in the economy. In a society in which specialisation of labour and production has advanced to a considerable degree, money provides a useful tool for measuring value and regulating exchange.[8] For an individual—or an organisation—the receipt of a monetary income makes it possible for him to determine his own priorities for expenditure. Thus money is a most effective means for delegating responsibility and providing freedom of choice. At the same time it simplifies the decision-making process by allowing the decision-maker to exclude from his consideration all criteria except his own priorities.[9] Because money widens choice it also provides an enhanced incentive for work and enterprise.

3

For society as a whole, in a situation in which the supply of goods and services can rarely meet the potential desires of the population, supply and demand can be brought into equilibrium by the operation of a competitive price mechanism which rations goods and provides an incentive for efficiency. In this way it seemed to nineteenth-century economists that the competitive market economy both maximised individual choice and provided an automatic system for co-ordinating the mass of individual decisions. As Samuelson puts it in a modern textbook for students of economics: [10]

> A competitive system is an elaborate mechanism for un-conscious co-ordination through a system of prices and markets, a communication device for pooling the knowledge and actions of millions of diverse individuals. Without a central intelligence it solves one of the most complex problems imaginable, involving thousands of unknown variables and relations.

To nineteenth-century economists, intervention in this system, by limiting competition, artificially restricting supply or controlling price, though providing often temporary advantages to some individuals, was regarded as basically harmful to the prosperity of society as a whole. This was considered true of both internal and foreign trade.

Limitations of the laissez-faire market economy[11]

In their reliance on the economic market as a means of distributing resources and co-ordinating decisions, nineteenth-century classical economists and their followers failed to recognise the importance of a number of weaknesses in the system. Some of these weaknesses were at the macro-economic level affecting the general efficiency of the whole economy: some at the micro-economic level governing the supply and demand for particular goods and services. Many of these weaknesses were becoming evident by the end of the nineteenth century, though their full significance might not become manifest until well into the twentieth century. They are related first to the effects of a policy of delegation

4

and second to the limitations of money as a measurement of value.

One of the functions of the economic market, as has been pointed out, is to simplify decision-making by delegating responsibilities to individual consumers and productive organisations. But the delegation of decision-making to low levels in a system makes certain sorts of decisions difficult to take and so limits possible lines of development.

The great advantage of any system of delegation is that it simplifies the decision-making process by putting decisions in the hands of those in closest touch with the working situation. This is particularly valuable where flexibility is required in meeting complex situations, and can usefully be contrasted with the inflexibility associated with hierarchical bureaucratic systems. So that giving an income to responsible parents is likely to be more effective in supplying family needs than bureaucratic decisions about the issue of standard rations and clothing. But this simplification of decision-making can only be made at the cost of increasing the number and importance of 'externalities'—that is to say issues that cannot adequately be evaluated within the terms of reference of the person making the decision.

There are many examples of externalities in the operation of the economic market. Both costs and benefits can be externalities, although most attention is usually directed to costs. Typical examples are the cost to others of pollution of the atmosphere or water system by manufacturing processes, transport systems, or urban living; the cost to all users of transport from delays and inconvenience as more vehicles are put on the roads; or the betterment that accrues to neighbouring areas as a result of an improvement in the amenities of a particular district. Perhaps the most important example of externalities created by an extreme *laissez-faire* system is the costs thrown on workers, their families and society as a whole by the refusal of employers to accept any responsibility for their workers other than paying them the market value of their labour. The maintenance and improvement of the quality of the labour force requires that workers receive an income that can purchase housing, food and clothing adequate at all times 'for the maintenance of merely physical health' for themselves and their dependents—to use Rowntree's phrase,[12] —together with health, educational and training facilities that will enable them to meet the demands of an industrial society. By the end of the nineteenth century it was clear that a laissez-faire system on the British or American models could not meet these criteria. The postulates of the economists, that labour could be treated like other factors of production with supply and demand brought into equilibrium by price, was shown to be short-sighted as well as being inhumane.

Within the economic market delegation to individual but interdependent units also creates uncertainty because some decisions depend on estimating the way in which large numbers of other individuals will make their decisions. This uncertainty in turn contributes to instability in the processes of production and growth, demonstrated by the regular cycles of expansion and depression in the business cycle. As a co-ordinating mechanism the economic market always tends to equilibrium, but the level of economic activity at which equilibrium is attained without external intervention may be far below what is technically possible.[13]

Uncertainty also affects decisions involving major changes in production. Classical economic theory in fact came increasingly to concentrate on the role of the market in determining 'marginal' changes in production and consumption.[14] Major changes could only be accounted for in terms of the 'entrepreneur',[15] whose role was to take the risks inherent in the uncertainties of the market. The need of the entrepreneur to control uncertainty has been an important influence in the drive to enlarge businesses, extending control over the resources required for production, and the outlets for the sale of products, creating monopolies and diversifying products. By all these means the 'perfect' market, whose competition provides the rationale of the classical economic system, becomes less and less a reality.[16]

Some of the problems of co-ordination and externalities created by delegation could be dealt with by voluntary agreements, for instance joint action to raise wages, or deal with pollution. In practice securing joint agreement among numerous independent groups or units is extremely difficult, particularly where any one of them can gain an immediate advantage by disregarding the agreement, or by making use of joint facilities without paying a contribution—the so-called problem of 'the free rider'.[17]

Other weaknesses of a *laissez-faire* economic system are associated with limitations of money as a measure of value. First of all, only some aspects of social welfare can be measured in terms of money. The value of goods and services or other aspects of welfare that are not normally bought or sold can only be valued indirectly or even not at all. How do you value a life saved, or a limb lost, or the work of a housewife and mother? Some of these problems will be examined in more detail later,[18] but meanwhile it is important to note, that as with all the social sciences, too much concentration on what can be measured may mean that too little account is taken of the immeasurable.

Even within the economic market monetary value is not an objective criterion like weight or length. The monetary value placed on goods and services through the economic market varies as a result of changes in the value of money as a whole —the all too familiar problem of inflation. More seriously it also varies according to the distribution pattern of income and other claims on resources. If income is transferred from one group to another with a different consumption pattern, then demand for the goods bought by the first group will fall, and their price will tend to fall too. Similarly the price of the goods bought by the second group will tend to rise.

This relationship between price and income distribution presents the flaw in the attempts of economists to define a distribution of resources that would maximise welfare on the basis of the so-called 'Pareto-optimum'.[19]

Pareto argued that the point of optimum welfare would be achieved when no individual consumer could gain anything by further exchanges of goods and services with any other consumer. At this point 'the marginal utility' of all products for each individual—that is, the value to the individual of the last additional unit purchased—would equal the price at which the products were offered. Similarly an ideal production schedule could be determined under perfect competition by equating marginal productivity and marginal cost. However, the Pareto-optimum proves not to be a unique position for

7

there is a different optimum distribution for every different set of prices and therefore for every different division of income. One approach to this problem by economists has been to suggest that if the division of incomes is given by some other, non-economic, process, the Pareto-optimum will give the most efficient distribution of productive resources.[20] Unfortunately it is impossible to divorce decisions about production from decisions about the distribution of income, least of all in a *laissez-faire* economy. Thus the situation is circular. The Pareto-optimum in fact has to be seen not as a unique position of optimum welfare, but only as an indication of one set of criteria which must be considered in an overall appraisal. To claim more for it is merely another attempt to give a spurious objectivity to criteria of value which can only be justified in political and moral terms.

Finally the monetary value given to those goods and services that do enter into the economic market represents only the value of the satisfactions that people expect to get from their purchases at the time of purchase. This may not be the same as the satisfaction actually achieved, let alone of the benefit received.[21] This is partly a problem of ignorance. In some cases this is an ignorance that could be fairly easily overcome by a person with the will to do so, particularly where one is dealing with a type of decision which is often repeated such as in the choice of food or clothing. But many choices are very complex and require either more time and energy in the search for knowledge than people may be able or willing to give, or they require an ability to use the expertise of others. In these circumstances people may prefer to save time and effort by leaving the decision to others. In Dahl and Lindblom's phrase people 'may object . . . to facing price system agendas'.[22]

Apart from ignorance about immediate satisfactions and benefits from choices that are made, a major problem is presented by the need to balance present and future satisfactions. Here one meets the concept, long familiar to economists, of 'discounting the future', the tendency of people to give more weight to present satisfactions compared with future discomforts, than they would do if the future was felt with the same immediacy as the present.[23]

8

Democratic welfare capitalism

The development of welfare capitalism can be seen as an attempt to maintain the advantages of a capitalist economy, with its delegated decision-making, incentives for work and self-co-ordinating mechanisms, while correcting the problems that arise from its limitations. It can also be seen as an attempt to maintain as far as possible the *status quo* in the distribution of resources, while bowing to the most irresistible pressures for change.

If one considers the policies that led to the creation of the post-war welfare capitalist state, some of the new elements were as much concerned with supporting the capitalist system as with social welfare. Measures concerned with the maintenance of full-employment and the planning of the economy —at least planning in the 1960s if not in the immediate post-war period—can be seen as a modification of *laissez-faire* to make capitalism more effective within its own terms by reducing uncertainty and maintaining stability. Similarly the Industrial Training Act 1964 was designed to share costs and so improve the system of industrial training, which had been relegated to the position of an externality for individual firms to the detriment of industry as a whole.

Other measures were aimed much more at giving greater priority to social objectives. They were designed to cope with the externalities of the economic system, particularly those that created costs for families; to protect aspects of our culture that were undervalued by the economic system, such as the protection of the countryside and the maintenance of historical monuments; and to distribute resources with regard to 'need' instead of 'demand'. Here real conflicts emerge between the values of the welfare and capitalist systems.[24] Capitalism emphasises individual self-determination within a system in which self-interest is harnessed to the common good by using resources as an incentive to action. Resources are therefore distributed as rewards for contributions to the common good. The competitive attitudes and the inequalities that result are accepted as a reasonable price to pay for individual autonomy. In contrast the welfare system places primary importance on the distribution of resources according to need which in turn

9

implies an emphasis on equality. The main incentive to action is an appeal to altruism and the common good, rather than self-interest as such. Co-operation is stressed rather than competition. The paternalistic role of the expert as the arbiter of need has been accepted as a necessary corollary of the system, though this is increasingly being disputed. At its simplest level the conflict is demonstrated by arguments about the effect of social security benefits and high taxation on work incentives. At a deeper theoretical level the same ideological issues underlie and sustain the argument between such schools of thought as that of the economists of the Institute of Economic Affairs[25] and the social administration school led by Professor Titmuss.[26]

But economics is about the distribution of power as well as the distribution of resources, and it is in this field that democracy, the third element of post-war society makes its contribution. Democracy and *laissez-faire* capitalism both spring from the same ideals of individual freedom and responsibility so both stress the right and the ability of the individual to make rational choices in contrast to the paternalism of welfare. But individual power is weighted differently in the two systems. In democracy each vote is of equal weight, and votes are distributed equally. In the economic system units of money are also of equal weight, but their unequal distribution gives individuals unequal power. The gradual extension of the franchise throughout the nineteenth and twentieth centuries has provided a political power to counterbalance economic power, and this has been an important factor in enabling the welfare system to rise beside and within the economic system. *Laissez-faire* capitalism could hardly have been converted to welfare capitalism without the state first having become democratic. Yet the democratic system and the welfare system also have their conflicts. Mention has already been made of the fact that welfare is paternalistic in tendency. At the same time democracy by biasing decisions in favour of majority opinion may lead to the neglect of minority interests, which are important concerns of welfare.

Thus differences in the values in the three systems, capitalism, democracy and welfare produce differences in principles that govern the distribution of power and of resources.

Social administration and the study of the social services

The study of the social services in Britain, usually referred to as social administration, sprang originally from its place in the training of social workers. It concentrated on those services about which social workers needed to know in order to help their clients and to understand their own role. Sometimes this resulted in a confusion between social services, social service and social work. Even so eminent an authority as Penelope Hall fell into this confusion in her account of the development of the social services.[27] This confusion has been intensified since the social work services of local authorities have been concentrated in a 'social services department'. Gradually the services examined have widened and social administration has been linked with social policy. Again some confusion may have been caused by treating the study of the social services as synonymous with social policy rather than as a part of it. Social policy must be wide enough to include economic policy as well as a whole range of issues such as communal relationships and individual liberty which cannot be considered within the context of the social services.

Social administration is therefore concerned with the study of social services, those services in fact whose primary objective is to relate 'needs' and 'resources' rather than the 'supply and demand' of the economic market. This requires examination of the nature of resources, the concept of need, methods of distribution, and the institutions through which distribution takes place, including the economic market in so far as it has a place in this process. Problems of power, attitudes and values will also have to be considered because of the way they influence all the issues that are raised including the practical results of any particular measure.

In pursuing this analysis chapters 2, 3 and 4 examine resources, need and the distribution of resources; chapters 6, 7 and 8 examine the concepts of power and authority and their manifestation in the social services with special reference to professionalism and the position of the consumer; chapter 5 links these with a brief examination of the problems of coordination. For logical completeness there should also be a linking chapter on organisations, but these have been so well discussed in relation to social services in books such as those of Blau and Scott[28] and Gilbert Smith,[29] that it seemed pointless to give a relatively inadequate summary. For similar reasons the chapter on co-ordination is much more superficial than the subject deserves, its main purpose being to make certain points which seem to be inadequately dealt with in the British literature on social services.

Chapter 2
Resources, income and wealth

Summary of the argument

If needs are to be met, however they are defined, resources have to be made available for this purpose. This means 'real resources', that is goods and services not just money. This distinction between financial resources and real resources is particularly important in the social services, because natural or artificial restrictions in supply make price a poor indicator of value.

Resources can be divided into wealth and income. Wealth is important because it generates income. Income is important because it governs consumption. Thus the extent to which the needs of the people of a nation are met depends on the size of the national income and how it is distributed in personal incomes. In turn the size of national and personal income is a function of national and personal wealth. There are a number of difficulties in measuring the resources available to a nation and in comparing the allocation of resources to different individuals within it. These difficulties relate to the inadequacy of money as a measuring tool, particularly in measuring wealth; and the difficulty of defining income. There is a tendency to manipulate the definition of income in ways that favour particular groups, and to define the income of less favoured groups as illegitimate.

'Real resources'

It is often convenient to talk of resources in terms of money, but money is a symbol whose significance depends on the fact that it is exchangeable for 'commodities', that is goods and services. These are 'real' resources.

For a wide range of consumer goods and of services of an unskilled kind an increase in financial resources produces a commensurate increase in the claim over resources. Thus an increase in the rates of social security benefits gives an immediate proportionate increase in the real standard of living of the beneficiaries, at least until general inflation reduces the value again. Several factors contribute to this. First, the increase in demand for particular goods is likely to be small in relation to total supply, particularly as the supply of many consumer goods is organised on an international basis. Second, the supply of many of these goods can be relatively easily increased in response to an increase in demand without increasing production costs—in economic terms supply is 'elastic' and 'marginal cost' relatively stable. Third, the increase in demand for any particular commodity is likely to be limited by the fact that there are relatively close substitutes for most consumer goods, making demand 'elastic' as well as supply.

These conditions, elastic supply, mobility between markets, stable marginal costs, and substitutability, are absent in the supply of many real resources. Where this is so it may not be useful to think purely in financial terms. Examples can be found among many of the most important resources required by the social services, such as land, buildings and skilled labour, particularly professional skills.

Land as an economic resource has two characteristics which are of particular importance in determining its price and use. The total supply of land is strictly limited, and it cannot be moved.

In some ways the absolute limits on the available land are less significant than might be thought except in so far as social value is placed on having large expanses of land thinly populated and relatively underused for recreational and related purposes. If economic forces were allowed free play, as the demand for land for various purposes increased, it would tend to be used more intensively—e.g. replacing detached houses with large gardens with high rise flats—and land that had previously been uneconomical for particular purposes would be brought into use. However, the effect of this would be to raise the price of land and to transfer additional income or wealth to those who happen to own land.[1] Equally, of course, it is possible for the economic demand for land, and hence its value to fall, but this is not a risk that has frequently faced landowners since the war.

Limits on the availability of land become more important when its immobility is also taken into account. Because of this the location of land is an important determinant of its value. Location affects the personal and financial costs of many activities that vitally affect the quality of living. To site a hospital on cheap land far from the urban population that it serves increases the cost of attendance and visiting in terms of money and time and reduces social contacts with those living in the community. Living a long way from work increases transport costs and reduces the time available for either work or leisure. To move one's home far from friends and relatives reduces intercommunication and mutual help.[2]

The immovability of land also means that what is done on one piece of land may have considerable effects on the value of neighbouring land and the buildings on it. The house purchased for its seclusion and salubrious air may be changed completely by the building of a nearby factory. But equally improved facilities such as parks and transport provided at public expense may increase its value. Such improvements in value are known as 'betterment'.[3]

The recognition of these factors and their important effect on the quality of life has resulted in Britain in a relatively strict control over land use. A side effect of this has been that the granting of 'planning permission' for a change of land use has often been a permit to make large profits, made larger by the artificial scarcity of competing land created by control elsewhere.[4] One reason for the Labour government's creation of the Land Commission in 1965 was to collect for the use of society as a whole such profits and betterment created by the action of society.[5]

Because location is an important aspect of the value of land, and many facilities need to be concentrated in areas where communications are good, social services often have to compete with commercial interests for the use of land in certain areas. This may result in heavy financial costs.

Unlike land, buildings and capital projects such as roads and sewage schemes can initially be put where it is believed they are wanted. But once built they cannot be moved, and they become almost a part of the land itself. They can only be demolished, and a new project built elsewhere. Unlike land

15

again, but like most capital goods, they are relatively specific to particular purposes. It is true that buildings set up for one purpose can be used for another, but there are usually heavy costs in adaptation, and they are often less efficient than when purpose built. Not only are buildings specific to a purpose, but they are often specific to the methods and way of life of a particular time. Their long life can in this respect sometimes be a handicap, since the existence of a well constructed building may be a disincentive to replacement, so that prisons, mental hospitals and workhouses of the nineteenth century still remain in use despite their total unsuitability for modern conditions.

The price of a building is closely related to the price of land, which may represent a very high proportion of total cost. This is true of both new and old buildings, and means that the price of buildings is affected by the same factors that influence the price of land. In addition, building production, because of the methods and organisation of the building industry, cannot generally increase fast enough to meet rapid increases in demand. So that there is also a more limited scarcity value attached to building itself. As a result of these conditions, increases in the availability of money for the purchase of, for example housing, by stimulating demand are likely to be dissipated in higher prices rather than increased production.

The greatest demand on resources made by the social services is the demand for labour and particularly a wide range of skilled labour of a kind that is usually called 'professional'. Labour, unlike other resources, cannot be treated merely as a means to an end and manipulated to that purpose. This was one of the errors in the reasoning of some of the classical economists.[6] Labour means people. Humanity demands that their needs are also considered and if this is not recognised the people concerned will ensure, openly or by subterfuge, consciously or unconsciously, that some attention is paid to them.[7] In this lie the seeds of a basic conflict between the social services and their employees. Such conflict may be particularly relevant in the case of 'professional' workers, an issue that will be discussed in a later chapter.

Although labour is never wholly specific, the skills of labour often are. Because employment is an important area of life round which many aspects of people's self-image is structured, people are often strongly committed to the use of particular skills, and this may make their labour very specific in character. One might expect that the more educated people are, the greater the range of work that they could undertake, and therefore the less specific their labour would be. This is only partially true, because of this commitment to the particular status of particular skills.

One particular kind of skill that is important in the social services can be subsumed under the heading of 'love'. When one talks of a person's need for love, whatever we mean by 'love', it must be conveyed by a person with the capacity to give love to that other person.[8] 'Love', normally springs out of a sense of common identity based on shared experience and the ties of blood. In this sense it may be very specific in its operation. One of the problems of the social services is to find enough people who naturally possess that capacity to love in a less specific form, who are capable of giving love to a broader range of people or who can do so if given a better understanding of people and their emotional needs. Unfortunately the importance of this skill is rarely recognised in a way that gives it adequate reward in the economic market.

Like land, the total of available labour in a country is limited, but it is equally possible to make more or less intensive use of the labour. For example a general expansion of demand can be met by increasing overtime, and by drawing in to the labour market more married women, more old-age pensioners, and more physically and mentally handicapped workers. A depression in demand can be met by the opposite process and also by raising the school leaving age—an irreversible process. The labour supply can also be increased or decreased through immigration and emigration. A general increase in the labour supply may still leave a shortage of particular skills, especially where there is a need for a long and expensive training, or where restrictions on entry are maintained by the existing labour force. Both factors have for example affected the supply of doctors, and particularly consultants in the National Health Service.[9]

Income and wealth

In estimating available resources it is customary to make a distinction between wealth and income. In the financial accounts of organisations this is reflected in the difference between capital and current accounts. Wealth and income tend to generate different psychological attitudes in our society. Wealth is something one tries to maintain; income is what is available for consumption. However, income and wealth are not necessarily mutually exclusive, and their relationship is complex. This relationship is presented diagrammatically in Figure 1. In the following discussion the figures in brackets refer to items in Figure 1. The argument is summarised in the explanation that accompanies the Figure.

Wealth can be defined simply as property (2), or resources already in existence. However, the importance of wealth lies in its potential for producing or realising income. So for some purposes the definition of wealth should cover not only property but what the classical economists called the factors of production (items in column A). The three basic factors of production are land (2a), labour (1a) and capital (2b) defined more broadly than normal usage allows as follows: [10]

> *Land* comprises all the untouched and primal dispositions of nature. . . . *Labour* means people of any and every kind, with all their various bodily and mental powers and skills. *Capital* means all other 'real' resources. . . . Since we have included under 'land' everything that owes nothing to man's efforts, all the kinds of things which come under the heading of 'capital' are man made.

Two other factors contributing to production may also be worth adding to this list—organisation (1b) and knowledge (1c) —though they are generally neglected as separate categories by economists because the return to them can rarely be distinguished from the return to labour and capital.

'Organisation' is an abstract concept distinct from the concrete 'organisations' within which it is demonstrated. It may be defined as established patterns of interaction which enable co-operative and interdependent activities to take place. Such patterns of interaction take time and effort to develop and it is often cheaper and quicker to use an existing system for some productive purpose than to create a new one. A clear example of saleable organisation in the economic market is the goodwill of a business. Within the social services the value of 'organisation' may justify the use of existing voluntary organisations to perform statutory functions or the extension of existing statutory organisations to take on new functions. Of equal relevance are the costs created by the disruption of existing communities and family patterns through redevelopment and other means.

Knowledge may be less important because it is taken into account in the valuation of skilled labour of which it is an integral part. Nevertheless it is a resource which exists independently of particular people. It can be bought and sold or even stolen, withheld or distributed freely, and its control is an important source of power.

The definition of income is more difficult than the definition of wealth.[11] To distinguish income clearly from wealth—existing resources—it can be defined as the current production of goods and services—the marginal increase in resources or the marginal product (items in column B excluding contributions from 7). But just as the importance of wealth lies in its relationship to income, so the importance of income lies in its relationship to consumption. In the absence of wealth—in its more restricted sense of property—income determines potential consumption. But wealth not only generates income through new production. It can also be turned directly into income either by sale or by increasing current production at the expense of maintenance or replacement—in effect allowing a capital asset to depreciate (7a).

The interrelationship between wealth and income is even more complex than this. Income is the product of wealth, but wealth is also the product of income in the sense that accretions to wealth depend on using income for investment rather than consumption. At the same time the value attached to items of wealth is largely determined by the income it is expected to generate, whether by the production of other goods, by appreciation of value as against consumer goods or by a direct contribution to the standard of living. This value is influenced by short-term as well as by long-term expecta-

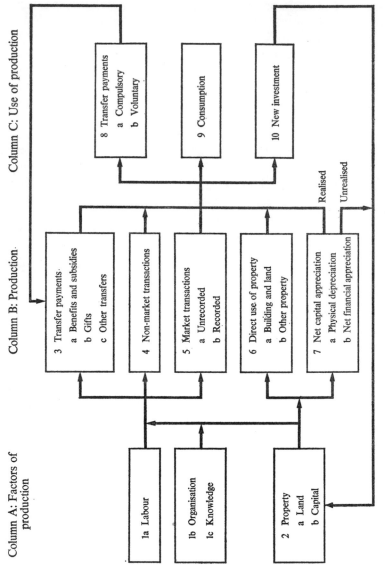

FIGURE I *Income and wealth*

Figure 1 is intended to show the relationship between wealth and income and the elements that may be included in different definitions of income: *wealth* is usually defined as property (2)—land and capital resources of varying degrees of durability. It may also be legitimate to count as wealth the investment in the skills of labour (1). Income is the product of wealth by this definition. *Income* is normally defined in one of three ways: as consumption (9), as net marginal product i.e. consumption plus new investment including, for individual income, savings (9+10), or as total increase in command over resources (9+10+ elements of 7 not already included in 9 and 10). Transfer payments (3, 8), that is payments made without any direct economic return like gifts and taxation, end up as part of someone's real income but should not be included in the income of both payer and receiver. For practical reasons non-market transactions (4), like the services of a wife and mother, unrecorded market transactions (5a) like jobs done 'on the side', and the benefits accruing from the direct use of property other than buildings and land (6b) are not usually included in income though they may in fact represent a significant proportion of personal and national income. Perhaps the most complex element in the figure is net capital appreciation (7). Physical depreciation (7a) is the 'real' depreciation which generally accompanies both use and non-use of property. Real income can be increased in the short run at the expense of capital by neglecting to maintain property or by extra heavy use of it as well as by the use of irreplaceable resources such as coal and oil deposits. Net financial appreciation (7b) is not a 'real' increase, in the sense that the property remains in its previous state. It is an increase in the monetary value of property in comparison with the monetary value of consumption goods, as for example when the prices of houses increase by 20 per cent when the price of consumption goods rises on average only 10 per cent. This net increase in value may be 'realised' by sale of the asset or 'unrealised'. In either case it increases (or decreases if there is a net loss of value) the command of the owner over resources but is not generally recognised as part of income.

tions, hence the rapid fluctuations that sometimes occur in the prices offered for industrial shares and similar investments.

This complex relationship between income and wealth leads to three broad approaches to the definition of income, each with its own validity for different purposes. The first approach is to define income in terms of consumption (9). This is particularly relevant to the comparison of standards of living. A second approach concentrates on the marginal increase in resources and includes, in addition to consumption, new savings (in the case of personal income) and new investments $(9+10-7)$. This type of definition makes a clear distinction between wealth and income, has a deep psychological appeal, and has a practical value in that it is in the allocation of new resources that there is most opportunity for making new decisions. The third type of definition of income is in terms of the increase in the total command over resources $(9+10+7)$. This includes the net increase in the value of the existing stock of wealth, due to its appreciation in value against consumption goods (7b), as well as the marginal increase in resources. Such a definition makes possible a broader comparison of the effect of changes in the distribution of resources on the life situation of individuals or nations.

Each of these definitions can be applied to income at all levels from the person to the nation or state, including intermediate systems such as families and organisations. At each level operational versions of the broad type of definition tend to vary in detail in the way in which particular items are treated. Income in kind, or items of income that do not normally pass through the economic market (4, 6b), like the work of mothers and housewives, are frequently excluded if only because of the difficulty of setting a value on them. Unrecorded market transactions are by definition impossible to include (5a). Certain forms of savings may be excluded in calculating personal income, as in taxable income or the concept of 'take-home pay' which excludes compulsory payments for insurance and superannuation. Tax payments may be included or excluded. The real depreciation or appreciation of capital assets may be more or less faithfully reflected in the items that are included.

Finally an explanation is needed of the term 'transfer payment' (3, 8). A transfer payment is one which is made without any direct economic return like a gift or a tax payment. To avoid double counting, these should be included in the income of either the payer or the receiver but not of both. For practical reasons compulsory transfers such as taxation and maintenance payments for a separated wife are usually included in the income of the receiver, voluntary transfers such as gifts and uncovenanted subscriptions to charities in the income of the payer.

National wealth and income

Accurate information on the value of national wealth would make possible an estimate of the basic strength of the economy, a check on information about the distribution of wealth and, above all, a truer picture of national income that took into account net capital appreciation. However, no official figures are prepared, in this or any other country. Revell[12] has published an account of his own work in the calculation of the wealth of Britain in the years 1957 to 1961, showing clearly many of the methodological problems involved. At the end one must still have many doubts about the light that his figures throw on the issues listed above. The market value of assets reflect their current rate of return and the current mood of the market as well as long term potential. The value of the skills of labour is excluded, although investment in skills is a valid alternative as well as a corollary to investment in capital. Many of the costs of production, particularly environmental pollution are not reflected in market valuations.

Because of the inadequate information on wealth, national income has to be calculated in gross terms ignoring the problems of depreciation. Its calculation therefore has to approximate to the second of the three types of definition, the marginal increase in resources available for current consumption and investment. Gross national income can be calculated in three different ways: by adding up all incomes excluding transfer payments: by adding up the value of all products; or by adding up all expenditure. In practice the two methods used are the income and the expenditure methods. The first gives the Gross National Income (GNI); the second the Gross National

Product (GNP). Since the expenditure of one person is always the income of another, the Gross National Income should by definition be equal to the Gross National Product, when appropriate allowance has been made for transactions with other countries. So the two terms are often treated as synonymous, although they give very different information about the distribution of income.

The GNI is calculated on the basis of the return to the factors of production before taxation and other transfer payments take place. Income for this purpose is divided into four broad categories:

1   Rent, profit and interest
2   Incomes of the self-employed
3   Wages and salaries
4   National Insurance contributions.

This division does not make possible an estimate of the proportional return to the three main factors of production, land, capital and labour. For example the income of the self-employed includes an element of profit—the return to capital —and an element for the return to labour, while the rents of land and of buildings are not separable from one another or from other profits. Nevertheless the figures do give some indication of the importance of employment as the basis for the initial distribution of resources. For example during the 1960s income from employment and self-employment together with National Insurance contributions which must largely be attributed to employment, accounted for approximately 75 per cent of the GNI. These figures of course understate the financial return to capital by omitting the value of appreciation. They also give no indication of the distribution of real income, if only because of the effects of taxation and transfer payments.

From many points of view information about the GNP is more valuable than information about GNI. Both give a picture of changes in the total of current production and, since they are largely derived from different sources they provide a check on each other. But the GNP also gives information about the nature of production, its distribution for instance between investment and consumption, between food, housing and health services and about the distribution of control, between personal consumers, industrial and commercial enterprises and government.

In considering changes in the distribution of production and in making international comparisons care has to be taken to remember the limitations of the figures for the GNP. First, they take no account of goods and services that are provided without monetary payment or for which the monetary payment is not recorded. This produces an underestimate of real national income, which will vary from country to country and affect international comparisons. Countries which rely more on subsistence farming, or make greater use of the extended family for the provision of services, or have a greater resistance to paying taxes are all likely to underestimate their real income to a greater extent than other countries. In considering changes in the distribution within a country this is of little importance to the extent that such practices remain constant. But if they do not remain constant, if, for instance, there is an increase in the number of working mothers with either a decrease in the services they provide for their children or an increase in paid services for children like day-nursery staff, the figures for the GNP will overestimate the value of the increased product.

Similarly some changes in the amount of money spent on certain goods and services may not be reflected in equivalent changes in quantity or quality. Such changes are particularly difficult to monitor in the provision of services.[13] The services of government employees like teachers or doctors are valued for inclusion in the GNP on the basis of the salaries paid. If better services are provided at the same cost, or worse services at a higher cost, the increase or decrease in real income will not show in the GNP. No one can tell, for example, whether the increase in expenditure on social-work services since the social-services departments were created in 1971 underestimates or overestimates changes in the quality of service provided. Most observers seem to think that there has been an immediate deterioration in the quality of service provided though they hope that this will be reversed. Neither change could be deduced from figures of expenditure.

Perhaps the most important limitation on the figures of the

GNP and the GNI is the fact that they are gross and do not take into account the effects of capital depreciation. They do not show for instance how far the expenditure on new housing in the post-war period was nullified by a deterioration in the quality of an important section of the market for privately rented property.[14] Perhaps even more important may be the depreciation of the environment through various forms of pollution which is an externality that does not appear in anyone's accounts.

Over the years since the Second World War, the figures for the GNP for this country and other western industrial states, have shown a steady increase in government expenditure both absolutely and as a proportion of GNP. Within this total there has also been an increase in expenditure on the social services.[15] This increase has sometimes continued even though particular governments have deliberately tried to keep down the increase in expenditure. For example the Conservative government of 1970 revised the forward estimates of expenditure inherited from the Labour government so as to keep increases in government expenditure below the expected increase in the value of the GNP. However the largest savings were in transfer payments such as subsidies to agriculture and industry and Godley and Taylor have shown that the revised programme still showed a proportionate increase in government claims on real resources.[16]

These increases in the monetary resources devoted to the social services almost certainly reflect some improvement in the relative quality and quantity of the services provided, but the value of that increase in real terms is difficult to estimate. Some at least will be compensating for environmental and capital depreciation, and probably for a reduction in unpaid services due to the break-up of communities and extended families, thus affecting the value of the net gain.

Personal wealth and income

The people of a nation live close to one another in situations in which their interdependence is manifest. So the distribution of resources between them is an important focus of attention, and has substantial consequences. Because capital gains and non-market transactions are a major contribution to differences in standards of living, the definition used for the calculation of income is of even more significance at this level than at the national level. In addition to the problem of defining income other problems also arise. What is the most important *income unit* to use—the individual, the nuclear family, the household or the extended kinship group? What is the *maintenance unit*—who shares in the income? What is the most appropriate *time unit* to consider—whether what is at issue is the income received in a week, in a year, or over a lifetime?[17]

The problem of defining the *income unit and the maintenance unit* does occur to a minor extent in the calculation of national income and wealth. For example decisions have to be taken about how to treat capital holdings of Britons abroad or of foreigners in Britain; and transfer payments to and from immigrants and emigrants. However, at a national level the value of the most important of these is generally known with some measure of accuracy and the effect of their inclusion or exclusion can be calculated. Where information is least accurate, errors will only make a small proportionate difference to the estimate of the national income. At the personal level the lack of clarity in the boundaries of these units is far more important in its influence on the calculation of income per head.

In many ways the most convenient unit for calculating income per head is the household. Within the household so many of the factors that contribute to real income are shared in ways which make it very difficult to separate the income of individuals within the household. For this reason the household is actually used as the unit of study in the so-called annual *Family Expenditure Survey* which provides the most useful information we have on comparative standards of living.[18] It is also used in the estimation of housing needs, and, in a modified form, in the calculation of eligibility for many benefits.

One limitation of the household as a unit of study is that it is not a wholly stable unit. It has temporary members, and temporary absentees, and there is always a problem of how to treat these. Moreover it is always open to a member of the household to leave permanently, if he feels that the contribution that is required of him outweighs the benefits he receives. This was a particular criticism of the household means test used to administer unemployment assistance in the 1930s. The requirement that the whole income of adolescent children should be taken into account in calculating the benefit received by their parents reversed the customary pattern of dependency in a quite unacceptable way, and encouraged the adolescent children to leave home. More recently attention has been drawn to the problem of how to treat the income of a cohabitee when calculating the entitlement to supplementary benefit of a woman without a husband to support her.[19]

Perhaps the basic problem lies in the fact that in an industrial society income accrues to individuals, while property is also generally owned by individuals. There is an expectation that personal income should be shared with a wider group which has some claim for the support of the income receiver. This expectation is backed by custom and indeed the expectation arises out of custom, but only in specific circumstances and to a limited extent does the custom receive the sanction of the law. A man's legal obligations are limited to the maintenance of his wife and his natural or adopted children. A woman has a similar obligation to maintain her husband and her children, but the former only if he is unable to maintain himself.[20] Even these limited obligations are difficult to define or to enforce. This is recognised by the matrimonial law which states that a maintenance order cannot be enforced so long as the husband and wife are cohabiting. While it is always open to the wife to end cohabitation by refusing to share a bedroom with her husband, and to prepare his meals, short of this she cannot enforce her maintenance. Even when separation has been achieved, the enforcement of orders often presents insuperable difficulties. For example among recipients of supplementary benefits with court orders or other agreements for the maintenance of themselves or their children, half the orders for separated wives, and one third of the orders for mothers with illegitimate children are paid irregularly or not at all.[21] It is in this context one must consider how realistic it is to enforce financial responsibility on those who have no legal obligation at all.

In general the tendency of social-service practice since the Second World War has been to bring the definition of income and maintenance units closer to the legally enforceable obligations of the nuclear family. Thus children over sixteen are entitled to supplementary benefit in their own right, and the earnings of members of the household other than the parents are ignored except for a contribution to rent. But there are many exceptions to be found in the administration of the services, often based on the view of the family as a unity which is denied by the individual basis for the receipt of income.

In the field of income tax the income and maintenance unit has never been based on the household, but on either the individual or the nuclear family. Moreover there has always been some possibility for at least wealthy taxpayers to choose between family or individual assessment. This has made it possible in a progressive system, to redistribute income by for example creating trusts for children of the family, so as to reduce the liability for tax. This sort of manipulation has not been possible for the recipients of welfare benefits without a physical splitting up of the family.

In the calculation of national income the minimum *time unit* has to be the year in order that effects of seasonal variations are adequately taken into account. Longer units of multiples of a year can be used, but if a useful purpose is served by this the calculation is not difficult if figures for the single years are used as the basis. In the calculation of individual income a much wider range of time units is possible. Many calculations may be based on a time unit as short as a week, while for some purposes the life income of the individual may provide the most relevant comparisons.

For taxation and for social service benefits the time units used for the calculation of income are of a year's duration or less. Different time units are used for different purposes. For income tax the financial year is the time unit. For supplementary benefit the relevant unit is income in the current week. For family income supplement it is income over the last five weeks. The effect of the short units is to discriminate between those with reasonably stable incomes and those with irregular incomes. Under a progressive tax system based on a short time unit those with irregular incomes will tend to pay a higher proportion of their income in tax. This is because the higher rates of tax paid in periods when their income is high will not be fully compensated by reductions in tax when their income is low.[22] On the other hand they are likely to become eligible for more means-tested benefits than those with a similar average income which is more stable. The shorter the time unit the greater the discrimination that will occur. Whether those with irregular income will benefit or lose from a short time unit depends on how their income varies in relation to the means test base and the income level at which taxation become progressive. However, one must also take into account that eligibility for benefit does not necessarily mean that it is received. There is considerable evidence that at present many of those who are entitled to means-tested benefits do not receive them. This is partly due to ignorance, partly to apathy, and partly to public attitudes to the legitimacy of such incomes. For example in the 1966 survey of the circumstances of families, almost a half of the families living on an income below the national assistance level were entitled to claim assistance but had not done so.[23]

Since irregular earnings are most likely to occur among manual workers, it is this group that is most likely to suffer from a shortening of the time unit for income tax purposes. The gains from a short time unit for means-tested benefits may be nullified by their reluctance to make repeated claims.

Time units of a year or less are of particular relevance to taxation and a social service provision that is geared to short-term emergencies. For a comparison of life chances it is income over the life span that is most relevant. Salary earners have greater opportunities to spread income evenly over their lives through superannuation, sickness and redundancy schemes. This helps to disguise the extent of the differentials between different types of work. It also reduces the incidence of taxation as a proportion of income.

Turning to the definition of income, it is clear that numerous different approaches are used for different purposes.

Figures for wage and salary rates, and gross earnings by occupation and industry are regularly collected by the Department of Employment and Productivity.[24] These figures have only a tenuous relationship with the real income of individuals and families, because they are collected to serve purposes dictated by the economic market and not welfare. They include money subsequently deducted for taxation which varies for each case. They exclude all those factors outside the employment situation which affect income as well as aspects of employment such as the employers' contributions to welfare through superannuation, sickness and similar schemes, income in kind and the conditions under which employment is undertaken. The latter should be considered as an integral part of an individual's standard of living though they rarely are. For example the conditions of work of a university lecturer, a school teacher, an official of the Department of Health and Social Services dispensing supplementary benefits, a worker on a car assembly line and a miner represent very different standards of living. Moreover, as Wootton has pointed out, wage levels do not generally compensate for these conditions, but rather the lower the wage, the worse the conditions under which it is earned.[25] Neither is any account taken of what might be considered as the net disinvestment involved for the person—the extent to which the nature of the work affects his health, involves risks of accident or death, or conversely provides opportunities for personal development. The figures for earnings can however be used to locate groups of people who are particularly at risk of enduring a low standard of living, despite being in employment. It therefore also makes possible a consideration of how their position can be improved.[26]

If one is concerned with a comparison of standards of living, information on expenditure is particularly useful. Such information is collected annually in the *Family Expenditure Survey*.[27] This takes the household as the income and maintenance unit, and the week as the time unit. The information is classified by the composition of households. By giving average expenditure on different types of goods and services it shows how different income levels affect the expenditure patterns of families. Information gathered in the survey has also been used to calculate the effect on income of taxation, social service benefits, and certain occupational benefits. The figures of household expenditure do not however give any picture of the influence of the use of capital goods on the standard of living. The quality of housing for example is only reflected in the levels of rent and mortgage repayments which are a very poor guide to quality. Similarly expenditure on long lasting goods such as bedding and furniture is no indication of the quality of life provided by existing possessions. One of the greatest problems faced by retired people and others who live for long periods on a reduced income is the steady decline in the serviceability of such goods, and the difficulty of replacing them. Many of the comments on items excluded from figures of earnings also apply to figures for expenditure, which ignore certain forms of income in kind, certain forms of savings, and net capital gains.

The concept of 'take-home pay' can be considered intermediate between gross earnings and expenditure. It is psychologically very important because it sets the limits on the immediate choices open to the recipient. It gives a better approximation to expenditure than does the figure for gross earnings, but in other respects suffers the limitations of the latter. As an indicator of standard of living it is crude compared with an expenditure survey, particularly in ignoring other forms of income, the effect of overheads such as rent, and the size of the maintenance unit.

Figures for taxable income before and after the deduction of income tax were once relied on as giving an authoritative picture of changes in the distribution of income. Since Titmuss attacked the validity of these figures in *Income Distribution and Social Change*[28] they have been used with much more caution. They suffer from inadequate definition of the income unit, the maintenance unit, and of income itself. They use the year as the time unit. Because these definitions are vague, and it is in the interests of those who supply the information, particularly in the higher income brackets, to manipulate the definition and the sources of income to make it appear that their income is as low as possible, there is a bias in the figures whose degree it is impossible to estimate.

The only figures that we have for the distribution of wealth are also collected through the Inland Revenue.[29] In this case they are derived from the evaluation of wealth for death duties. Like the equivalent figures for income distribution they are biased by the tendency to manipulate the distribution of capital so as to avoid the payment of tax. Revell considers that the effects of such manipulation on the figures has been exaggerated, but other limitations also arise because the total distribution of wealth is derived from a sample composed of those who happen to die in a particular period. This sample is also likely to be biased, and the effects of this can only be partially allowed for.

Income and means tests

In calculating income for determining eligibility for means-tested benefits there is considerable variety in the way different elements are treated. Many of the variations are the result of compromises springing from basic dilemmas in the operation of means tests.

The first dilemma is provided by the choice between simplicity and comprehensiveness. In order to be completely fair between one applicant and another, as many factors as possible that affect real income should be taken into account. This should include such special needs as the cost of a medically prescribed diet or extra fuel for a cold or damp house, and such overheads as the cost of fares to work and hire-purchase payments. But the more needs are taken into account the more complicated the assessment becomes. This results in more complicated forms, more personal questions which may be resented, and more difficulty for the applicant in knowing beforehand whether or not he is eligible for the benefit. All this discourages applications and means that people who are eligible are less likely to apply.[30]

Then there is the problem of how to treat capital. For tax purposes capital is ignored except for its contribution to income through interest or realised capital gains. Even lump sum cash payments under superannuation schemes may be ignored for tax purposes provided they do not represent too high a proportion of the benefits received. In means tests too capital is generally ignored up to a certain level in order not to discourage people from saving. Beyond that level it may be treated as though it was an annuity. For example under the Ministry of Social Security Act 1966[31] the first £300 of capital was ignored in assessing entitlement to supplementary

33

benefits. For the next £500 an income was assumed of one shilling per week for each £25 of capital. This is rather over 10 per cent per year and will generally involve some supplementation of income by using capital. With capital over £800 an income of 26 per cent was assumed, which would involve substantial dissaving. Equally the Supplementary Benefits Commission, like the National Assistance Board before it, will not make payments that contribute to the capital of a recipient. So they will not take into account repayments of capital owed under a mortgage, but only the interest payments. Yet from the point of view of the recipients the mortgage payments may be as much an unavoidable overhead as rent is to tenant families, and rent is met in full. In taking this line the Supplementary Benefits Commission follows the Inland Revenue, and also the Department of Education and Science in calculating the parental contributions to the maintenance of students in institutions of further and higher education. Many other means tests treat mortgage repayments as the equivalent of rent.

The problem of the treatment of capital, as has been indicated, is partly a problem of incentives to save. Means tests also raise problems of incentives to earn.[32] If there are clear cut off points in the assessment of eligibility, loss of benefits may cancel out to a greater or lesser degree the advantages of increased earnings. If all income is taken fully into account in assessing eligibility, the effect may be similar to a 100 per cent tax rate. This is often modified by disregarding some proportion of income from other sources. For example in the assessment of supplementary benefits, up to £1 or £2 per week of income from other sources may be disregarded in calculating benefits, but above that all income is taken fully into account, including the assumed income from capital outlined above. For recipients of the National Insurance retirement pension in the first five years after they have become eligible, earnings up to a certain figure are disregarded. Above this half the value of earnings (but not unearned income) is deducted from the pension, thus giving an effective marginal tax rate on earnings of 50 per cent. The family incomes supplement produces a similar 50 per cent tax over the income range to which it applies.

While incentive effects may be allowed for in the calculation of most benefits individually, the accumulated effects of the loss of several benefits over a similar range of income is generally ignored. It has been shown that this can produce very high notional tax rates even exceeding 100 per cent when liability to income tax is also taken into account. One local authority, Barnet, devised a scheme for taking into account multiple contributions to local authority financed benefits, but this could not take into account national benefits, and has not found general favour with local authorities.

Income in kind is generally ignored in the calculation of income in means tests, but it sometimes seems to affect benefits. For example a lower rate of supplementary benefit is paid to non-householders compared to householders. This is justified on the grounds that householders have greater financial responsibilities, but also seems to take account of the contribution of householders to the real income of non-householders. Cresswell and Parker for instance, quote the case of a single unemployed man who found his supplementary benefit reduced when he moved into his mother's house so that he could care for her.[33] A similar attitude is reflected in the reassuring comment in the Government survey of the *Financial and other Circumstances of Retirement Pensioners* that most pensioners not receiving supplementary assistance even when they might have been entitled to it, had an income that enabled them to live at least as well as those who were receiving it.[34]

In conclusion one can say that the variety of definitions of personal income used in taxation and in the assessment of eligibility for benefits is partly due to a valid response to specific problems. But much more important is the lack of a clear policy co-ordinating these different measures. This is particularly evident in the conflict between the tax and the benefit systems.

Because income is inadequately defined there are opportunities for manipulation. Taxpayers can manipulate income to reduce tax liability. Those who administer benefits can manipulate eligibility requirements to reflect specific prejudices. A prime example of this appears to be demonstrated by Marsden's study of unsupported mothers receiving supplementary benefits.[35] He found that the real incomes of these mothers tended to vary according to their social status, widows having higher incomes than separated wives, and separated wives higher than unmarried mothers.

The legitimacy of income

Just as the definition of income can be manipulated to favour particular groups, so attitudes to the legitimacy of income can serve a similar purpose. Full legitimacy gives an unquestioned right to the receipt of income and freedom in its use. Illegitimacy means that the right to the income is conditional and freedom in its use is curtailed.

In law a clear distinction can normally be made between legitimate and illegitimate income. This dichotomy does not accord with the attitudes of society. People make much finer distinctions in evaluating the legitimacy of income from different sources, and these may conflict with legal definitions. The evaluation of different forms of income may also vary between different cultural groups and different individuals.

There are a number of indicators of social attitudes to the legitimacy of incomes from different sources. These include the extent to which conditions are attached to the use of the income; the physical and other conditions under which it is given; the certainty of receiving it without humiliation; the sort of investigations used in detecting illegal receipt and penalties imposed for its discovery; the criticisms levelled against those who receive the income; and the willingness of people to ask for or accept it.

The source of income which has the widest acceptance in our society, and also has the highest legitimacy rating is income from employment. The right to receive it is unquestioned; the right to use it in any way the recipient wishes is unrestricted except for certain legal and customary liabilities for the maintenance of wife and children.

Income from property and wealth is generally regarded rather similarly to income from employment, but its acceptance as legitimate may not be quite so wide. Those who receive profits, rent and interest are more likely to be subject to criticism on the grounds that they do not give an adequate return for what they receive. Unearned income is taxed at a higher rate than earned income. While the formal justification for this is based on the fact that earning income involves increased expenditure, it seems likely that public acceptance of the distinction is based on a concept of legitimacy.

'Earned rights', such as those provided under the National Insurance scheme have a legitimacy close to earned income, but there are variations even within this scheme. The right to retirement pensions is rarely questioned; but the sick may be accused of malingering and the unemployed are often regarded as 'layabouts'. The payment of unemployment benefit has a time limit unlike sickness benefit.

Universal benefits like family allowances and the National Health Service also seem to have a wide measure of acceptance. However, the reluctance of politicians to raise family allowances to keep pace with increases in the cost of living, may reflect doubts about the attitude of the public.[36] There are also uncertainties about when one has a right to call on the services of a general practitioner, which may not arise under private practice.[37] This suggests that a service provided free even under these circumstances may have an ambiguous legitimacy.

There are many indications that means-tested benefits have a lower legitimacy than almost any other kind of income that is not specifically criminal.[38] The attitudes of those who administer the benefits, especially those closest to the recipients, the condition of the premises in which they are administered, the public belief in major abuse, the attitudes of those who are eligible, whether they claim or not, all reinforce each other in stressing the negative social attitudes to this form of income. Even here distinctions may be made between different types of recipient. Pensioners, the sick and the unemployed provide a similar hierarchy, though perhaps at a lower level, in supplementary benefits as in national insurance. Comment has already been made on Marsden's findings for widows, separated wives and unmarried mothers.[39]

Cutting across the relatively clear hierarchy of legitimacy in these contractual or statutory types of income, is the question of support from relations, friends and neighbours.[40] There is a reluctance to ask for help where this may be refused or given without enthusiasm. There is often a reluctance to accept what is offered freely if it is feared that an unspoken debt or inferiority or dependence is implied. Money cannot be given as freely as goods, or goods as freely as services, perhaps because of differences in the likelihood that the recipient will be able to make an adequate return. So today the resistance of children to taking into their homes their elderly parents may sometimes be less strong than the parents' fears of the loss of their independence.[41]

Pinker relates the stigma attached to various forms of income to the theory of exchange.[42] Income for which a return is or has been made is more acceptable than that provided without return. This is clearly of major importance but it is not the only issue involved. Obviously the value judgments also reflect definitions of deviance, and suggest an element of scapegoating.

Chapter 3
The definition of need

Summary of the argument

The definition of need presents a central problem for the social services, since this defines the objectives of the services. To speak of a need is to imply a goal, a measurable deficiency from the goal and a means of achieving the goal. The goals may be set by some sort of consensus within society, by the person in need ('felt' need), or by experts with a knowledge of specific means for achieving particular aims. An alternative classification of definitions contrasts the 'normative' definitions of society and the experts with 'felt' need and with 'comparative' approaches based on 'average' standards in the population.

Another way of looking at the same problem is to consider first the difficulties of defining ideal goals, such as 'health' and 'optimum personal development', and then at attempts to operationalise such ideal norms. Five operational definitions are considered: basic minimum standards, comparative need, felt need, definitions in terms of specific techniques and national need. An examination of these approaches suggests that each has limitations springing from implicit assumptions about what can or should be changed. Ideal norms tend ultimately to be defined in terms of adjustment to the environment, which from other perspectives can itself be the subject of change. Minimum standards imply assumptions about the maintenance of the *status quo*. Comparative definitions which have developed from minimum standards are potentially very radical because of the extent to which they point to an egalitarian distribution of resources. Felt need is limited by the knowledge and expectations of the subject which may be unrealistically optimistic or pessimistic. On the other hand the expert who uses specific techniques has too limited a knowledge of other methods to make a valid differential diagnosis.

Widening the concept of need to take in the possibility

39

of broad changes in the social and economic environment leads to the concept of 'national need'. While this widening of the framework of change makes it possible to consider quite radical positions, governments, on whom such changes are likely to depend, are for practical reasons likely to be biased towards policies that maintain the fundamental *status quo*.

If the validity of any definition of need is to be assessed, it is essential that the limitations of the particular approach adopted should be understood, and the underlying assumptions spelt out as clearly as possible.

The elements of need

If the meeting of need is the objective of the social services, the definition of need is vital to their understanding. Nevertheless, as Walton[1] pointed out, little attention has been given in the literature of social administration to consideration of this concept. Slack,[2] for example, following Titmuss, only makes use of a crude classification into short-term and long-term needs. Walton noted that although the term 'need' is often treated as though it referred to an objective fact, its definition always involves questions of values. The assertion that X has a certain need involves three separate statements: X is in state Y; state Y is incompatible with the values held in society Z; therefore state Y should be changed. The first of these is a statement of fact about which it should often be possible to gain agreement by an objective examination of the evidence. Agreement about values is more problematical. Even when reached our present state of knowledge in the social and biological sciences leaves room for considerable argument about the effectiveness of different forms of ameliorative action, particularly in the long run. Thus room is left for disagreement about values and the goals that stem from these, and also about the means to achieve these goals.

Walton's exposition of the nature of need makes it clear that he regards the values of society as decisive criteria for need. This perhaps makes the problem seem too simple. Clearly in western industrial societies it is the diversity of values that seems most evident, and the values that determine the needs to be met by the social services, or at least their priorities, are as likely to be set by an activist minority as by a general consensus. Walton himself later in the same article, puts forward the case for greater emphasis to be given to 'felt' need, that is to say the need expressed by the recipients of services. Almost by definition these are minority groups, since even the consumers of the broadest services like health, social security and education, have different felt needs in relation to these services.

In addition to society as a whole, and the consumers of services, a third group has an important role in defining need. This is the experts, those with special knowledge about particular areas of need. These experts may help society or the state in clarifying its own definition of need, or perform the same function for consumers. In either case the definition that emerges is likely to be strongly influenced by the expert's own perspective. This perspective will generally be based on his understanding of particular methods and skills. By concentrating on such specific techniques, it is possible to avoid the need for agreement about long-term goals, and the difficulty presented by our ignorance about the relationship between specific means and these long-term ends. This approach is particularly attractive, because of the way in which it simplifies the agenda for decision-making.

The approach of the expert to the definition of need like an approach based on the values of society, can be regarded as 'normative', in that the standards are set from outside in contrast to the concept of 'felt' need. A third type of definition relies on a comparison of the standards actually achieved by different groups within a society. For example, it may be regarded as inappropriate for income levels to fall below a certain proportion of the average national wage. Or again provision of facilities for the handicapped may be designed to enable them to maintain a way of life that compares reasonably with that of those among whom they live. This has been called 'comparative need'.

A useful way of examining different approaches to the definition of need is to start by considering various ideal norms that have been put forward as goals for the social services.

Once the difficulties of defining such ideals precisely have been recognised it is possible to examine the advantages and disadvantages of various ways of operationalising such definitions.

Ideal norms

Need is often assessed in relation to ideal norms such as 'health', 'personal maturity' or 'optimum personal development'. One practical difficulty in using such goals is posed by the problem of individual differences in potential and in the use that is made of what is provided. In the fields of education this can be seen in differences of opinion about the importance of genetic factors in setting limits to individual potential as well as the personal and social factors that affect response to different forms of educational programme. In the field of nutrition there are individual differences in absorption rates and in requirements for the maintenance of health about which little is known.[3]

Of more fundamental importance is the difficulty of defining the goal itself. Even in a subject like nutrition, in which we have come to expect considerable precision, this is a problem. The diagnosis of deficiency diseases and diseases of excess presents no problem but almost nothing is known about optimum levels of nutrition. Paradoxically more is known about animals than about humans, because the goals for animals can be more clearly defined and little consideration is given to subjective feelings of well-being. This was a basic problem faced by the eugenics movement. It is possible to define quite precise goals for the breeding and feeding, of for example, cows. One breeding society aimed to produce a cow which would 'produce on average 1,512 lbs of milk solids a year . . . would have a high food conversion rate, be clean fleshed and early maturing'.[4] If the size of bust, waist and hips were really of primary significance in breeding and feeding our womenfolk we would have less problems, but for human beings maximum growth, early maturation, maximum resistance to disease or long life are a few among many alternative criteria.

The problems of defining the ideal norm is well illustrated by the World Health Organisation definition of health as 'a state of complete physical, mental and social well-being and not merely the absence of disease or infirmity'.[5] This draws attention to the close relationship between physical, mental and social conditions in the situation of the individual but in encompassing almost every aspect of living becomes almost meaningless. Either it involves a concept of happiness which will vary from culture to culture, or it becomes merely a question of adaptation to the environment. But this leaves open the possibility that the environment itself may be patho-genic. The clearest example of the effect of adaptation to a pathogenic environment is provided by institutionalisation. In its most extreme form, institutional neurosis, there is a recognisable pathological syndrome which can be diagnosed even within the institution,[6] but in other cases it is only when the inmate comes out of the institution that the results may be recognised. If the culture of a whole society is involved, it may be very difficult to know who is more healthy, the person who adjusts or the person who does not. These problems are particularly relevant to the definition of mental health, and have provoked much discussion.[7]

An ideal norm which has been very influential was developed from Bowlby's work on maternal deprivation. Bowlby postu-lated that 'what is believed to be essential for mental health is that the infant and young child should experience a warm, intimate and continuous relationship with his mother (or permanent mother-substitute) in which both find satisfaction and enjoyment'.[8]

Bowlby's conclusions were criticised by Wootton on a number of grounds, but the core of her argument was that Bowlby concentrated too much attention on the question of separation, and not enough on the quality of care provided both before and after the separation.[9] But it was an anthropolo-gist, Mead, who drew attention to the cultural bias implicit in the conclusions.[10] She pointed out that in primitive societies unwanted children generally do not survive. This sometimes results from cultural patterns, such as the burying of the new-born child with its dead mother. Or it may result from a natural biological response to the failure of the child to thrive, with failure of the breast milk followed by an increased failure of the child, mediated by the mother's anxiety. In our society

43

there is a strong cultural emphasis on survival, and the impersonal concern for the survival of the child contrasts with a reluctance or inability to provide the personal care and attention that is necessary for the child to develop. Mead further summarises the evidence from studies of children brought up communally in kibbutzim and in Hutterite communities, which suggest that in kibbutzim the children become excessively dependent on the peer group and among the Hutterites on the community. She concludes 'Neither of these bodies of data suggests that children do not thrive and survive under conditions of group nurturing; they both suggest, however, that their mobility and flexibility are impaired.' Mobility and flexibility are of course values of considerable importance in our society, but clearly need not be universal values.

Mead's position still makes it important to define personal care and attention. An attempt to operationalise this concept has been made by Raynes, King and Tizard,[11] who have devised a scale based on Goffman's concept of the 'total organisation'. This attempts to measure aspects of institutional care such as rigidity of régime, block treatment of inmates, depersonalisation and staff inmate interaction. Children's homes cluster round the lower end of the scale and hospital wards round the top, showing maximum institution-orientation. While from some points of view this looks like a form of ideal norm, it can also be seen as a minimum standard, for once the grosser differences are eliminated, much more subtle differences in the quality of care and its effects on children are likely to be discovered.

Minimum standards

One of the most familiar approaches to the operational definition of need is the concept of the minimum standard. Walton quotes with approval Rowntree's attempt to define a subsistence minimum.[12] Rowntree himself was well aware of many of the subjective decisions involved in his definition. In the first place, in defining a minimum standard one must still begin by defining the goal to be achieved by the standard. For Rowntree the goal was 'the maintenance of merely physical health', and he deliberately ignored expenditure 'needful

for the development of the mental, moral and social sides of
human nature' or even for sick clubs and insurance.[13] This
was not of course because he regarded such matters as un-
necessary but rather that they were difficult to measure and
were not needed to make out his case for action. Even the
concept of 'merely physical health' was primarily directed
towards participation in the economy. The food requirements
for adult men were such as would provide sufficient calories
for 'moderately heavy employment',[14] and the clothes 'should
not be so shabby as to injure his chances of obtaining respect-
able employment'.[15]

Equally Rowntree knew that anyone living on this income
in the society of his day was unlikely to receive a diet that
would maintain his physical health by these standards. Inefficiency, misspending and culturally determined patterns of
expenditure, as for instance buying the more expensive animal
protein instead of the vegetable protein on which Rowntree
based his calculations, would inevitably see to that.[16] As so
often happens the concentration on a *measurable* scale diverts
attention from the real goals being sought.

In his later studies Rowntree made rather more allowance
for social expenditure but it was still meagre.[17] Beveridge's
scale was based on Rowntree's and its inadequacy was demonstrated by Townsend.[18] He showed that families living on such
incomes spent on average less on food than Beveridge considered that they needed. Since Beveridge's day participation
in the economy has come to be regarded as an inadequate
goal. A broader concept of social participation has been
accepted, involving family and neighbourhood interaction,
and higher standards of parental care. In an age of rising
standards of living such social participation is seen to depend
on having a minimum income that is related in some way to
the average and so on the avoidance of gross inequalities of
income.

At this point it becomes clear that the apparent objectivity
of the basic minimum standard disguises a fundamental political issue. One reason for having a 'minimum' standard is that
its achievement involves a minimum interference with an
existing situation. In the case of income maintenance this
situation is the distribution of income through employment

45

on the basis of established differentials and through the possession and transmission of wealth. These methods of distribution are regarded as in some sense 'normal'. Once their validity is called into question, so is the concept of the basic minimum.

A somewhat similar pattern of concepts can also be seen in other services besides social security and income maintenance. Minimum standards for housebuilding were established in the nineteenth century for housebuilding and for overcrowding.[19] A less clearly defined concept of 'unfitness' underlay plans for slum-clearance. These standards were based on an assumed relationship between bad housing and health which has never been clearly defined. Since the nineteenth century standards have been steadily raised. As with income the raising of these standards has been associated with the acceptance that style of life is as important to people as physical health. In 1967 the government undertook a sample survey of the condition of housing in England and Wales using three criteria for minimum standards: unfitness as defined in the Housing Act 1957; the possession of four out of five recognised basic amenities namely internal WC, fixed bath, hot and cold water system, and wash basin; and state of repair excluding internal decoration.[20]

These are standards for existing housing. An additional problem arises with new building. Houses when first built are generally expected to last for 60–100 years, to a period when minimum standards are likely to be very much higher than at the time of building. Since the first introduction of central government subsidy for local authority housing, the former has attempted to control the quality of public house building through the subsidy system. But since at many periods the main concern of central government was one of economy these standards have often failed to take into account the needs of the future creating a problem of inadequate housing for a later generation. In 1961 the Parker Morris Report[21] took this into account in proposing standards for future council houses which were regarded at the time as luxurious, including for example partial central heating at a time when central heating was still relatively rare. These standards were accepted as government policy in local authority housing in 1965, and encouraged, less effectively, for building in the private sector.[22]

In building for the future in this way a serious problem is raised about who should pay for these higher standards, the tenant who happens to enjoy them, although he might prefer something cheaper and less luxurious, or the community which requires high standards for its investment in the future.

Education too has had its minimum standards, though for some at least these have always been modified by ideal goals. The concept of 'elementary' education in itself implies a minimum concept, but this was compounded by Lowe's Revised Code of 1862 which made payment of a grant to schools dependent on attendance and the results of examinations based on the 'three Rs'.[23] Lowe's concern with establishing minimum standards was closely concerned with economy, that is with its immediate effects on the distribution of income, but the provision of universal education also roused anxieties because of its effect on the structure of society. Elementary education could be expected to have a minimal effect on this.[24]

One of the pressures for improved standards in education is the fact that education has an important investment component, affecting future productivity, and that as in house-building, one has to take into account the standards required of the current output in future years. Another similarity to housing is the division between a public and a private sector and the great difficulty in controlling minimum standards in the latter. Many private schools are still not 'recognised as efficient' by the Department of Education and Science.

In general the advantages and disadvantages of minimum standards tend to lie in the same qualities. A minimum standard involves a minimum interference with an existing condition, whether it is the current distribution of material resources, as in poverty standards, of status and privileges as in education, or of power as in minimum standards of provision imposed by central government departments on local government. Their validity depends on the weight attached to maintenance of the *status quo* or a relatively slow rate of change. Similarly another advantage of minimum standards depends on their clarity and the ease with which a shortfall can be measured. But focusing on the measurable leads to the ignoring of that which cannot be measured. So education may concentrate on examination results at the expense of wider goals; high rise

47

flats may fulfil all the Parker Morris standards without providing an adequate living environment; and people with adequate incomes may still have an inadequate diet.

Comparative need

Comparative definitions of need are an extension of basic minimum standards. The standard, instead of being set by criteria with a spurious semblance of objectivity, is related to average standards in the community. The standard set by a comparative definition can be quite low if a low proportion of average standards is taken as the minimum. But to make a comparison with the average is to invite questioning about the appropriateness of the level chosen, which can make no pretence to be other than arbitrary. Thus to state that retirement pensioners on supplementary benefits receive about one-third of average national earnings automatically raises the issue of why the proportion is so low. In this way comparative definitions can represent a particularly radical approach to the concept of need.

In education the concept of elementary education for the working classes has given way to the ideal of equality of opportunity. This implies a comparative approach at its most extreme. Equality of opportunity is not of course the same as equality of provision, since one of the functions of the education system is to select those who can be expected to benefit from additional provision beyond the average. But at the basic level it implies not only equality of provision but even 'positive discrimination'—discrimination in favour of those whose environment provides less support for the educational process.[25]

In the same way in provision for the physically handicapped the comparative approach to need requires the provision of a level of help which will allow them to enjoy a way of life similar to others in the community. At first this was interpreted in terms of the maintenance of personal independence, aids for living in the home, work opportunities, transport, income. Now the additional question has been raised. How much help and encouragement should be given to both the physically and the mentally handicapped in assuming con-

jugal and parental roles which may require substantial outside help to sustain?[26]

The comparative approach has been most explicitly used
in studies of 'poverty'. Comment has already been made on
the way in which Rowntree's concept of an objectively determined minimum income has been replaced by the concept
of a minimum income related to average earnings. But real
income is more important than monetary income as a determinant of poverty and this is reflected in a definition of
poverty made by a panel of the Social Science Research
Council.[27]

> Every generation has to rediscover and redefine poverty
> for itself. The most important contribution made by the
> latest reappraisal, here and in many other countries, has
> been to show that since the definition calls for an assess-
> ment of human feelings and relationships poverty must
> be measured in relative terms. People are 'poor' because
> they are deprived of the opportunities, comforts, and self-
> respect regarded as normal in the community to which
> they belong. It is therefore the continually moving *aver-*
> *age* standards of that community that are the starting
> points for an assessment of its poverty, and the poor are
> those who fall sufficiently far below these average
> standards. Their deprivation can be measured and their
> numbers counted by comparisons with the average per-
> sonal income (e.g. those receiving less than half this
> figure) or with a standard of living currently sanctioned
> by government (e.g. those living in unfit houses, and
> those with incomes less than the Supplementary Benefits
> Commission's scale rates) or with average life chances
> (e.g. those with sufficiently low IQ or school attainment,
> or mortality rates appreciably exceeding the nation's
> average). But 'felt' deprivations do not match the 'objec-
> tive' distribution of poverty at all closely: misery, mili-
> tancy, and poverty (like happiness, complacency, and
> wealth) are not very closely correlated with each other.

An even wider view of poverty is represented by Runciman's concept of 'relative deprivation'.[28] For this Runciman
turned to Weber who considered that to define adequately a

person's social situation, his position must be plotted on three dimensions; social class, social status and power.[29] Weber's definition of social class is different from that which is normally used, and which includes elements of status, and perhaps also of power. To Weber a person's class was determined by his membership of a group with common economic determinants for its life chances, or more briefly 'income' if 'income' is taken to include the source of income as well as its amount. Status refers to the respect with which people are regarded; power to the ability of a person to realise his own will despite resistance. So Runciman's historical study of relative deprivation considers changes in the income, the status and the power of the working classes.

Baratz and Grigsby[30] make use of a similar range of component concepts, though with a different nomenclature. They abandon firmly any definition that sees poverty as a 'lack of enough money . . . to buy a market basket of goods and services which, by society's standards must be consumed for enjoyment of a minimally "decent" standard of living'. Instead they consider that 'poverty' is best viewed as a condition involving those *severe deprivations* and *adverse occurrences* that are closely (but not necessarily exclusively) associated with *'inadequate economic resources'*. Thus the essence of poverty is seen to lie in the actual condition of life, not the low income that contributes to this condition. The deprivations and adverse occurrences that make up this condition of life are then classified under five headings :

> Severe lack of physical comfort
> Severe lack of health
> Severe lack of safety and security
> Severe lack of welfare values
> Severe lack of deference values.[31]

It is these last two that correspond to Runciman's use of lack of status and power as elements of relative deprivation. 'Welfare values' include all those elements that affect a person's self-perception, including for example 'inability to perform a socially valued function (e.g. paid work)' and 'lack of a good quality education'. 'Deference values' include those elements of a person's life situation that have a bearing on society's view of him and the extent to which he is taken into account in the acts of others, such as 'exclusion from participation in the political process (especially powerlessness)' and again 'lack of a good education'.

Baratz and Grigsby draw two important conclusions from this approach. First, that the measurement of poverty must be based on the use of particular indicators that show how deprivations and adverse occurrences are distributed among different income groups. Second, that policy needs to take far more account of the importance of the source of income in meeting the economic elements of poverty. A far higher priority should be given to employment as a source of income, because of its high legitimacy in American and British society. Beyond that the choice should always be biased towards the form of income distribution that involves least deprivation of welfare and deference values.

'Felt need'

A fourth approach to the assessment of need is to make use of the individual's own sense of need—his subjective feeling of discrepancy between what is and what ought to be. Walton[32] in discussing this uses the term 'felt need' a concept from the field of community development where the emphasis on voluntary co-operative activity makes the worker very dependent on the effective motivation of his clients.

The importance of felt need is recognised implicitly or explicitly in numerous situations within the social services. An emphasis on client motivation for change, as in community development, social casework and child-centred education is likely to lead to an approach based on felt need. Compulsory earnings related income maintenance schemes can be justified on the view that the subjective experience of poverty is as important as minimum standards for the determination of need, even though the compulsory element seems to throw doubt on the validity of the individual's judgment. Felt need is a necessary condition of self-referral on which many services are based. Those who seek to extend choice in the social services through a greater use of the economic market are also implicitly or explicitly laying stress on the importance of individual judgment in determining need.

However even those services like social work most dedicated to the ideal of self-determination, in practice only allow the client a limited role in defining the help he should receive. Lippett and his colleagues,[33] examining the role and function of 'change agents', such as psychotherapists, social workers and management consultants, noted the limitations in the client's perspective which justify the intervention of the change agent. On the one hand there is the distortion in the client's perception due to concentration on the pain and frustration produced by current symptoms, and to the reluctance to face the need for change. On the other hand the change agent has knowledge which is not available to the client. This knowledge covers the general cause and effect sequence that relates to symptomatic behaviour; the knowledge of how to fit this to the particular circumstances of the case; the knowledge of diagnostic procedures; and the knowledge of what can be changed and of techniques for doing this. This is true of other services, such as medical care.

Walton pointed out that a policy of provision based on felt need would require a wide dissemination of knowledge, and indeed a much greater openness about the criteria for decisions than most of those concerned with the provision of social services, professionals, administrators and representatives, are generally prepared to show. But one may be up against a much deeper attitudinal problem among potential consumers of the social services, whose belief in the possibility of change may be stunted by long experience of deprivation and of failure to achieve successful change. The effects of this have been examined in many situations. Runciman followed his broad historical study of relative deprivation with an attitude survey which showed that the poorest sections of the population were hardly aware of their poverty at all.[34] A study of poverty in St Ann's, Nottingham, concluded that the phenomenon of poverty among wage earners seems to be self-feeding, in that the lower a man's wages, the more deprived he appears to be, the less aggressively he will construe his needs, the less he seems likely to respond with either vigorous complaints or even active discontent.[35] Halsall and Lloyd's study of elderly patients admitted to hospital showed that more than two-thirds claimed they had been ill so long that they had forgotten what it was like to be well.[36] Roberts's study of entry into employment showed how young people's ambitions are based on occupations they expect to enter rather than their expectations developing from their ambitions.[37]

Definition in terms of specific techniques

As the definition of goals presents such difficulties, one of the commonest approaches is to abandon goals and to define need in terms of specific techniques available for change. So one talks of the need for housing, old people's homes, kidney machines, child care, social casework or supplementary benefits. This is particularly convenient for a social service system based on specialisation by process i.e. on the basis of particular skills, procedures or knowledge. It reflects the approach of the expert, whether professional or administrator. But as Lippett[28] pointed out in connection with the agents of planned change, the knowledge of the expert is not objective. His views of the subject matter for change will be determined by the techniques of change with which he is familiar, and these in turn will both affect and be affected by the cause-effect thesis to which he is committed and his diagnostic procedures. So the doctor is trained to ask the question 'Can this condition be improved by medical care?' which inevitably tends to produce a medical diagnosis and therefore a medical definition of need. He is not trained to ask 'Would this condition be improved more effectively by rehousing, psychotherapy, matrimonial conciliation, divorce or medical care or some combination of these procedures?', a question which he is not qualified to answer.

The definition of need in terms of specific techniques thus leads to a number of problems. First, there is the difficulty of making a general diagnosis which will bring into play the right range of skills. If a child appears apathetic in class, is this an educational problem, a medical problem or a social problem? How can a teacher know whether or to whom the case should be referred given his own limited frame of reference? Again, if a delinquency case is referred to a social case-

E

worker he will probably diagnose and treat a family problem; if it is referred to a community worker the diagnosis might be in terms of the cultural environment and the treatment would be based on this. Autism and severe subnormality were both defined at one time as primarily medical problems, and cases were placed in hospitals where they often deteriorated. Both have recently responded to redefinition as educational problems,[39] and severe subnormality to social care.[40]

A second limitation of this approach to need is posed by the fact that several needs frequently arise simultaneously. Several services and skills have to be co-ordinated in the client's interests. Traditionally there has been a tendency to leave this co-ordinating function to the client but he is likely to be lacking in both the knowledge and the influence required to perform this function.

Third, with alternative diagnoses available, it is extremely difficult to add up needs with a view to planning the provision of services. This is the more serious in view of the frequent absence of co-ordinating machinery between services organised on a specialist basis.

National need

All problems of need arise out of the relationship between individuals and their environment. So needs may be met by operating on either side of this relationship. The locus of change may be placed in the individual or in his environment or some combination of the two. The person who fails to manage on a low income may be taught more effective budgeting, or have his income raised or both. People whose mobility is impaired by accident or disease, may have their mobility improved by the use of particular aids or skills, or by changing the structure of their housing and of public buildings that they need to use.

The social environment is particularly important in its influence on the needs of individuals. The ways in which people meet their basic physical needs such as for food and sex are strongly influenced by social custom. People's sense of self-respect and self-fulfilment depend to a large extent on the relationships they have with others in their immediate environment. These relationships in turn are influenced by wider social attitudes both to particular conditions and behaviour—such as mental illness, physical handicap, illegitimacy and unemployment—and to the social order generally. Finally the needs of people are affected fundamentally by the structure of social institutions such as education, employment and politics. So for example an understanding of the needs of the elderly will move outwards from a knowledge of the physiological and psychological changes that to varying degrees affect the elderly. Factors that contribute to their social isolation, attitudes to the non-employed and the physically and mentally handicapped, barriers to employment according to their actual ability will all be relevant. So will the way in which economic resources are distributed among individuals. Hence the importance in understanding need of some acquaintance with the range of the social sciences, but particularly with psychology, sociology and economics.

The earlier examination in this chapter of definitions of need has concentrated on concepts of individual need. Focusing on individuals or minority groups encourages the placing of the locus of change in the individual or in what one may call his local environment, which in any case seem easier to tackle. So psychological and family approaches to the control of delinquency are more readily implemented than sociological approaches partly because delinquency comes to notice through individual cases, and partly because sociological explanations may require a much more fundamental restructuring of the institutions that regulate access to opportunity. But the individual approach may be no more than a palliative for a fundamental social problem. The same issue is raised by arguments about the role of social casework as opposed to community work and social reform in dealing with the social problems of individuals and families.

Large-scale changes in the physical, social and economic environment, if they are to be consciously directed, require government action. The general policy of nineteenth-century British governments based on their concept of the national interest was to avoid intervention in the social environment, leaving decisions to individuals and the forces of the economic market. The earliest interventions in the field of social welfare, apart from the Poor Law which they had inherited from an earlier period, were in fields such as public health, the education of a literate work force and the maintenance of law and order where national interests were clearly at stake, and the individual pursuit of self-interest had equally clearly failed. Even the Poor Law was restructured in a way that would intervene as little as possible in the operation of the economic market in the supply of labour. The story of the development of the welfare state is the story of the gradual recognition of the importance for the nation of positive policies with regard to the social and economic environment, and a widening of the concept of national need to include the welfare of all citizens and inhabitants of the national territory.

National need can be regarded as the sum of the needs of the individuals composing the nation including their joint interest in survival as a nation and the maintenance of the cultural heritage. If one adopts a view of society which emphasises the common interests of its members, as some sociologists have done, then this is a useful approach. But an alternative view of society recognises the importance of conflict between the interests and needs of different groups and classes.[41] In the narrower field of individual welfare this is not only a matter of conflicting priorities, between for instance the claims of an élite on the grounds of its contribution to society and the claims of the socially deprived on the grounds of their need; it is also a matter of absolute conflict, for instance between the needs of social rejects to be integrated into society, and the need of those whose interests require separation from such elements of society. Of course the wider the implications of changes that are being considered the greater the likelihood of their provoking widespread conflict.

National need is potentially a very radical concept because of the way in which it widens the framework within which individual needs can be considered. In practice it may be very conservative. First, government decisions about priorities are likely to be strongly influenced by the existing structure of power. Second, governments are likely to be activated by a desire to avoid conflict. Both of these factors are likely to result in a bias towards maintaining the *status quo* or at least in a democracy only supporting those changes that have very wide public support. Finally there are many factors which will encourage general public support for conservative policies.[42]

Conclusion

Each of the approaches to the definition of need that have been considered has its own advantages and disadvantages and its own peculiar validity. Ideal norms provide a general aim which by its wide acceptability is often useful as a spur to action. But their very generality limits their value in determining precise objectives and progress towards those objectives. Minimum standards make possible a clear measurement of deficiency but their apparent precision may disguise a failure to achieve the real objectives of the programme. Comparative definitions combine an ideal of equality with some of the precision of minimum standards. Felt need is justified as a criterion for action by the importance attached to the subjective feelings of persons. These four all have more to say about goals than about means to achieve the goals. Definitions in terms of specific techniques avoid decisions about the broad issues involved in establishing social goals by concentrating on known means of change. In this they have a certain precision, but may, like minimum standards, deflect attention from the real objectives of action. The concept of national need makes possible the consideration of much wider changes in the social and economic environment.

Yet the fundamental limitation of all approaches to the definition rests on their assumptions, often implicit rather than explicit, about what can and should be changed. If the validity of any definition is to be assessed it is essential that the underlying assumptions should be spelt out so that the limitations can be understood.

Chapter 4
The distribution of resources

Summary of the argument

Different ideals of social justice imply different principles for the distribution of resources. The primary method of distribution in our society is based on the ownership of property and employment which emphasise status and merit rather than need as criteria for distribution.

There are a number of different channels that are traditionally used for the distribution of resources. These include the economic market, the family or household, the local community or neighbourhood, mutual benefit associations, philanthropic organisations and the churches. On the whole these traditional channels reinforce a distribution related to status and merit. The only major exceptions are philanthropic organisations. When the state makes use of traditional channels for the provision of social services, it may reinforce this tendency unless it selects appropriate means to counteract it.

Redistribution can take place in various directions; over the lifespan of the individual, between individuals, between present and future, between geographical areas.

Redistribution over the lifespan is the form of distribution that intervenes least with the principles of the economic market. Redistribution between individuals may take place between different income groups—vertical redistribution—or between income groups with the same income but different needs—horizontal redistribution. These forms of income redistribution may be contrasted with 'contingency redistribution' where the meeting of specific needs regardless of income is the main objective. 'Universal' services are directed to contingency redistribution, and any income effect is due either to the way the contingencies met are correlated with income, or to the impact of taxation. Selective services are *ipso facto* income redistributive. However the choice between the two depends less on this than the value attached to distribution through the economic market rather than the welfare system.

Redistribution over time involves investment either in capital resources or in education and training.

The aim of equalising provision in relation to need in different geographical areas has been termed 'territorial justice'. Territorial justice relates particularly to inherited capital investment, current resources of skilled personnel, and current financial resources for investment and consumption. Provision of a service by central government is likely to result in greater territorial justice. Most services, however, are provided through local authorities with a large measure of autonomy. The present method of distributing central government grants to local authorities has counteracted the most blatant effects of the maldistribution of current financial resources. Other geographical differences are only marginally influenced by central government at the present time.

One of the functions of price in the economic market is to ration scarce resources between claimants. In the absence of realistic prices, in the social services rationing has to be performed by other, frequently irrational means.

Criteria for distribution

The primacy of property ownership and labour as the normal basis for distributing claims on resources is so generally accepted in our society that the validity of other criteria is often not recognised. Yet even in our own society other criteria are commonly used and in other societies they may be dominant.

Runciman has put forward three commonly accepted definitions of social justice in the distribution of resources: [1]

There are, broadly speaking, three different and mutually incompatible theories of social justice: the conservative, the liberal, and the socialist. In the conservative theory, social justice consists in a social hierarchy, but a hierarchy governed by a stable system of interconnected rights and duties. Those at the top are the holders not merely of privilege but of responsibility for the welfare of those below; and through the recognition that different strata

59

in society have different functions to fulfil, the hierarchy is accepted without dissension or envy as long as the responsibilities imposed on each class are in fact properly exercised.

In the liberal theory, by contrast, there is also a hierarchy; but this hierarchy is only legitimate if it has been arrived at from a position of initial equality. The liberal is not against inequality, but against privilege. He demands equality not of condition but of opportunity. He places a value not on an élite of caste, or inherited culture, but of individual attainment.

The socialist theory, finally, is the strictly egalitarian theory. It may or may not require as a corollary that the state should play a predominant part in economic affairs. This is really only a means to an end—the maximum of social equality in any and all its aspects.

In our present economic system we start with a distribution of property that is influenced as much by status, through inheritance, as by economic merit. Neither is earned income by any means determined solely by economic demand though need still has a low priority. Wootton[2] examined the criteria used in the adjudication of wage disputes and found that economic criteria were little regarded as determining the limits within which certain negotiations took place. The importance of status was demonstrated by the use of outside comparisons and the acceptance of differentials established by tradition. Merit was recognised in promotion within a career structure rather than in the payment of basic grades. Need was only considered marginally relevant in the determination of the rates for the lowest paid and in relating increases to rises in the cost of living index. Routh's study showing the consistency of sex and class differentials over a period of sixty years tends to confirm that view.[3] Routh concluded, 'The outstanding characteristic of the national pay structure is the rigidity of its relationships'.

However, even more important in our society in discussing need as the basis for distribution of resources is the high proportion of the population that lacks any bargaining power in the economic market at all. In 1971 only 25 million out of a population of 56 million were 'economically active' and the distribution of wealth does not compensate for this.

Channels of distribution

Apart from the various institutions of the economic market there are several other channels that are traditionally used for the distribution of resources. They include the family, or household, the local community or neighbourhood, mutual-benefit associations and philanthropic organisations. The churches are also important, displaying at different times the characteristics of each of the last three types of institutions. They serve the needs of their own members; they act as philanthropic organisations serving others in need, and they often act as a central forum for the concern of the local community.

The traditional channels for distribution, if uninfluenced by the state, in general tend to reinforce the broad structural differences in the distribution of resources based on status and class rather than need. This can be seen most clearly in the economic market and the family for rather different reasons.

Where social services such as medical treatment, insurance and housing are purchased in the economic market, it is obvious that distribution will tend to be highly correlated with the distribution of monetary income and wealth. When they are provided by an employer as part of the system of remuneration, provision also tends to be more generous for those who are higher in the hierarchy and those who are more highly paid. For example not only are employers' pension schemes generally proportionate to earnings, but they are more common for non-manual than for manual workers, for men than for women and for retired workers rather than their widows.[4] Many other types of provision in kind through employment also tend to follow a hierarchical pattern; subsidising of cars through mileage allowances, payment during sickness and entertainment allowances. Where housing is provided under the terms of employment, as in government employment in the former colonies, the quality tends to be related to the style of life considered appropriate to a particular rank. This tendency to relate occupational benefits to status has perhaps been exaggerated by the British tax system which has generally fallen lightly on payments in kind, and so has encouraged highly paid employees to seek part of their income in this form, but it also follows the logic of the economic system.

In contrast to employing organisations, the family or household is far more likely to be oriented to a distribution of resources based on need, though perhaps with a tendency to overestimate the needs of male earners and to underestimate the needs of mothers and housewives.

However, families, and particularly nuclear families, are small bodies whose limited membership and sources of income affect their ability to provide coverage for exceptional needs. Their access to resources is closely correlated with social class and employment. Poor people in fact generally have poor relations. At the same time needs and deprivations of different kinds tend to go together.[5] For example families with several children are, for whatever reason, more likely than smaller families to lack a father, and to live in overcrowded and insanitary accommodation.[6] Families without a father generally have a low income with all its concomitant deprivations, as well as lacking the emotional support that a father can give to the family. Chronic sickness and disability reduces income as well as increasing medical needs.

In the same way traditional institutions other than employing organisations and families are affected in their ability to meet needs by the pattern of their internal distribution system, by their access to resources, and their tendency to be divided on class lines. Mutual-benefit associations are oriented towards meeting need, but tend to exclude those potential members who present most risk. So the nineteenth-century trade unions and friendly societies were organised to meet the needs of groups of skilled workers, while the unskilled who were most subject to the effects of irregular earnings were excluded. Almost none of them had the resources needed to provide pension schemes. The Poor Law placed on the local community responsibility for the care of its own poor. In Elizabethan times these local communities contained both rich and poor living in close proximity. In the nineteenth and twentieth centuries urbanisation has separated the rich and the poor, so that reliance on the local community for self-help may again reinforce class differences.

Almost the only traditional channel that does not reinforce these structural differences is the philanthropic organisation, including the churches when they act in this way. Hence the importance of voluntary organisations and philanthropy when the state refused to take responsibility for social welfare. However even such philanthropy may help to increase status differences, by putting the poor under an obligation to the rich.

State use of traditional channels

When the state becomes concerned to give more emphasis to need in the distribution of resources, it can either use these traditional channels, or make direct provision itself. In the former case it may use encouragement, compulsion, material support or some combination of these three to gain its ends. Decisions about the channels and methods used will affect the distribution of benefits, and the distribution of costs. It will also affect the distribution of power, which is discussed in subsequent chapters.

If the state intervenes and uses encouragement or compulsion without the provision of adequate additional resources, it may be able to modify the internal distribution patterns of institutions, but it will not affect the problems created by inadequate access to resources and by divisions between institutions on class lines. There are many examples of this.

From 1911 to 1948 the national unemployment insurance scheme was restricted to manual workers and to non-manual workers with low incomes. The effect of this was to place a major responsibility for maintaining the short-term unemployed on those who were themselves among the poorest of the nation. After 1934, when employers and employees were paying a third each of the costs of the scheme, not only was a reserve built up to meet the needs of a future slump, but annual repayments were made on the debts incurred in earlier years.[7] During the same period public assistance was largely financed through the local rates so that the poorest communities had the highest burden to support. Estimates of need were based on the household and the earnings of older children were taken into account thus placing on children responsibility for the maintenance of their parents. The legislation of 1948 spread the costs for relief of sick and unemployed workers more widely by making insurance universal (though the flat-rate contributions were still regressive in their effect), by centralising responsibility for national assistance so that deprived communities were less penalised, and by treating children over sixteen as individuals in their own right.

Another example comes from the recent emphasis on community care in the provision of many services. By encouraging the family and the local community to accept responsibility for dependent and deviant persons, a better service may be provided, but it may not be a much cheaper service. The costs in terms of time, effort and stress as well as resources have been transferred from paid staff to unpaid families and neighbours. If there is really spare capacity this may be justified. But it may substantially reduce the quality of life of those who are in any case most deprived. One recent study, for example, has shown how care of the elderly has often devolved on other elderly people, who are little less infirm.[8]

If the new pattern of distribution imposed by the state contravenes too blatantly the accepted pattern, there is likely to be evasion, and problems of enforcement will develop. In the 1930s the household means test was widely believed to have contributed to the break-up of families by the departure of 'liable relatives' who were not prepared to accept responsibility under the household means test.[9] In the 1970s there is some evidence of evasion of the Equal Pay Act designed to improve the earnings of women.[10]

If the state channels additional resources through an institution without attaching conditions to their receipt, redistribution between institutions can be achieved, but the new resources are likely to be distributed within the institutions according to the established pattern. Subsidies to industry and agriculture may increase employment but the distribution within the productive organisations follows the normal pattern of distribution of economic institutions. The same is true of tax concessions in superannuation schemes. This is of course less of a problem if the distribution pattern of the institution is geared to the meeting of individual need as in the case of families, mutual-benefit associations and philanthropic organisations. However, even where the typical institution is appropriately oriented, some may be inefficient, like problem families, or atypical in their orientation.

An interesting example of the dilemmas of state intervention is provided by the different methods used to help families support their dependent children. Family allowances were introduced in 1945 to provide financial support for dependent children. The support was given through the family, and more particularly through the mother of the family, as the parent most likely to be oriented to the needs of the children. By using the family, it was possible for attention to be given to individual needs, but at the same time it made it possible for parents to misuse the money. Additional provision was made for children through school meals. These meals were provided at a subsidised cost, or, in case of need, free. However, the use of schools as the channel of provision also had its disadvantages. All children do not attend school; meals are not provided in all areas, or not in the quantity required; and many children dislike the meals, and prefer to eat at home or elsewhere. Many children who are entitled to free provision do not get this, and some families prefer to have their children home rather than undergo the means test that entitles them to free meals.[11] Several studies have suggested that in the 1960s the children who were most likely not to receive the meals came from poorer families.[12]

Types of redistribution

If government action is seen as changing the distribution of resources that would occur without that intervention, then the changes can be in various directions :

Over the lifespan of the individual
Between individuals
Between present and future
Between geographical areas.

Each of these deserves separate consideration.

Redistribution over the lifespan of individuals

The importance of redistribution over the lifespan of the individual was clearly demonstrated by Rowntree's discovery of the poverty cycle.[13] The single worker without dependents and the young married couple without children are comparatively well off. When children are born, the wife is likely to stop working, and the needs of the family to increase as the children grow in age and numbers. Later, as the children grow up and become more independent the demands on the parents' income are reduced and the wife may go out to work again. This comparative affluence lasts for a few years, but is terminated by a sudden drop in income at retirement. This may be followed by a slow deterioration in real income as a result of inflation and depreciation of capital. Superimposed on these cyclical changes may be short term changes in income due to sickness or unemployment.

Some redistribution over the lifespan can be effected by using the normal mechanisms of the economic market. This was the reason for the Victorian emphasis on saving; it is the basis for superannuation schemes and salary payment during the periods of sickness, and of some forms of insurance, particularly the insurance against unemployment and sickness pioneered by the trade unions and friendly societies of the nineteenth century. Since many of the situations which produce the need for such schemes have an uneven and unpredictable incidence in the lives of individuals, savings schemes are usually combined with an insurance element so that risks are shared.

The state has intervened in this field for a number of reasons. Some risks are uninsurable. No insurance company is likely to insure against the birth of children, while the decline in the adequacy of income that children bring comes before the long period of comparative affluence in middle-age, not after it as with retirement. The state assists through family allowances, and by reducing taxation while the children are dependent and increasing it when they no longer have to be maintained. The high costs of education are met from general taxation, and so are the high costs of medical care in old age, for which it is also very difficult to provide insurance.

A similar problem is posed by the support of widowed and separated wives. Pensions for widowed mothers, if covered by employment, are based on the relatively low earnings of early married life and not on the potential earnings of the deceased. Compulsory state insurance for widowhood at a standard rate is accepted, but not insurance against separation which, unlike widowhood, is felt to be under the control of the participants. Beveridge did propose that 'innocent' separated or divorced wives should receive an insurance benefit,[14] but this was not accepted in 1948, and does not accord with current views about responsibility in marital breakdown.

Just as some risks are uninsurable, through the economic market, so are some people—or at least may be so regarded by insurance companies. The chronic sick, the disabled, coloured immigrants and the elderly are particularly likely to come into this category.[15]

The tendency of people to discount the future may also justify state intervention, since the state is likely to have to meet the needs that result from such a failure of foresight. This can be met by compulsory insurance. But for many people with low incomes, failure to provide for the future may be justified by the real pressures of current needs. Just as they cannot afford private insurances, so compulsory insurance increases their poverty unless there is a significant transfer element in the insurance scheme from those better placed. This was the weakness of Beveridge's flat-rate insurance contribution which became effectively a regressive tax.

Distribution over the life-cycle presents certain practical problems. Money can be saved, but the consumption goods that are not purchased at that time as a result of the saving cannot normally be saved for future use. There are two alternative ways of dealing with this problem. The first is to invest the money saved in capital goods that will increase production at the future date. The second is to give up current resources for current consumption by others in need in return for a recognised claim on future resources.

This second form of provision for the future cannot normally take place, except to a limited extent, through the economic market—at least in so far as it does occur the future claims are likely in present circumstances to be depreciated by inflation. It has however always been the basis of intergenerational exchanges within extended families. The working generation has supported both its younger and its older dependent members in the expectation that similar support will be given when its members in turn reach old age. It is also the basis of the National Insurance scheme which, because it is guaranteed by the state, can, with a measure of certainty ensure that those who pay today receive equivalent value in the future.

Provision for the future by investment is also possible for the state, in the same way that it is possible through the economic market. But if it does this, the state will gain control of a steadily increasing proportion of the land and capital resources of the country—'nationalisation by the backdoor' as it is sometimes called. This would mean a substantial change in the power structure of the country. Whether this would be desirable or not is a matter of opinion, but such a change should come as a result of a deliberate political decision rather than as a side issue in a social-security programme. It is no doubt for this reason that the Labour Government was so cautious in its proposals for the use of the temporary surplus of contributions that would have resulted from the implementation of its superannuation scheme in 1970.[16]

Redistribution between individuals

State redistribution between individuals is generally regarded as being aimed at a transfer of income from rich to poor, or from higher to lower social classes. This is not necessarily the case.

Education, which takes about one quarter of the resources devoted to state social services, is strongly biased towards benefiting an élite group which is largely recruited from better-off families. Vaizey,[17] for example, estimated that in 1951 the annual educational subsidy per child in middle income groups was two-thirds greater than in lower income groups. A grammar school child throughout his secondary school career gained double the resources of a secondary modern pupil.

To a lesser extent the same is true of assistance to owner-occupiers in the housing market.

Much of the redistribution that takes place through taxation and the social services is a transfer between those with different needs but in the same income group. Examples are provided by income tax allowances for children, graduated benefits in social security, and superannuation schemes provided by employers and supported by tax allowances.

Webb and Sieve[18] analysing the processes of individual redistribution call transfers between different income groups 'vertical redistribution'. If this takes place from richer to poorer people they call it 'positive'; if in the opposite direction it is 'negative'. Transfers between those with the same income but different needs they call 'horizontal redistribution'. In all these forms of redistribution, the transfer of income between particular income groups is an essential element of the provision. Webb and Sieve call this 'income redistribution' as opposed to 'contingency redistribution' in which policies are designed to meet specific needs of people who may be in any income group. The National Health Service is an example of contingency redistribution. They point out that contingency redistribution is the only form of redistribution to arise from the provision of social services *per se*.[19]

In the redistribution of resources between individuals two broad alternative systems may be used, 'universal' or 'selective'. In a universal system services and benefits are provided to all those in need regardless of their wealth or income from other sources. Examples are the British health, education and national insurance systems. In a selective system services are provided to those in need only if their resources are insufficient to enable them to purchase the services through the economic market and monetary benefits are only provided to those with incomes below a minimum standard. Examples are free school meals and the supplementary benefits system.

Basically a universal service is directed to contingency redistribution. It will only have a major positive income effect if the contingencies it is designed to meet are negatively correlated with income, or if the costs of the service are met by higher taxation of those with higher incomes. In this connection it is important to note that the taxation system does not have to be progressive to produce an income redistribution effect. If contingencies are distributed evenly among different income groups, a proportional or even a mildly regressive tax system will have a positive income effect provided that the absolute amount of tax paid rises with income.

In contrast selective services are *ipso facto* income redistributive, so that it might be expected that those who are most concerned with ensuring greater equality in our society would favour selective services. In practice the opposite is generally true because of their concern about the stigma attached to the receipt of selective services and a failure to achieve a satisfactory level of take-up of these benefits. The strategy adopted by egalitarians is therefore on the one hand to improve universal services and finance them through higher progressive taxation;[20] and on the other hand to develop services to meet contingencies that are highly correlated with poverty, such as old age, or physical and mental handicap or the absence of one parent in a family.[21]

The development of a policy of income redistribution through universal and other contingency services can be regarded from one point of view as requiring more resources than a similar policy based on a selective system.[22] For example it 'costs' the state less to meet the needs of poor families through the selective 'Family Income Supplement' than through universal family allowances. But these are not real costs. They are transfer payments. The comparison between the systems can be put in another way. In a universal system a larger proportion of individual income—and therefore of the Gross National Product—is distributed through the welfare system instead of through the economic market. If the comparison is made in this way it can be seen that the expense argument is really based on a plea for the maintenance of the *status quo*, as with other situations in which needs are defined in terms of minimum standards. The real issues relate to the values associated with the welfare system and the economic market discussed in the first chapter, together with the practical and social difficulties associated with the administration of means tests and with redistribution through a system involving high taxation.

The importance of values in determining attitudes can be

seen in the position taken by Titmuss.[23] He accepted that the immediate result of introducing universal health services and secondary education after the war was to benefit the middle classes rather than the working classes. He also believed that the middle classes were able to make better use of the services provided, although in relation to health services his conclusions have been queried.[24] Nevertheless, Titmuss has always been a supporter of universal services because of their contribution to the quality of life of the deprived and the social ideal that they invoke.

The most complete evidence of the transfer of real income through the social services is provided through the publication by the government of a series of estimates of the distribution of taxes and benefits in different years undertaken by J. L. Nicholson of the Central Statistical Office.[25] The studies themselves and the criticisms of them[26] indicate the enormous complexity of making any valid estimate of this kind. The studies themselves are based on an analysis of data collected for the annual survey of household expenditure. Among the most serious methodological issues that arise are the problems of defining income and the income and maintenance unit as discussed in chapter 2 of this book, the problems of allocating costs and taxes, and the problems of defining and allocating benefits. The fact that the data are collected at a particular time and provide cross-sectional information means that the importance of distribution over the lifespan is ignored. The smallness of the sample also affects its reliability especially in considering minority groups.

Nevertheless these studies, despite their limitations, represent the best evidence we have of the redistribution effect of the social services. Year by year the picture they have given has been very similar, suggesting that at least the results have a measure of reliability even if their validity is in doubt. In general the British tax system seems to be mildly regressive at lower income levels and proportional over a very wide income range. Nicholson's figures also show taxation levels favouring those with children against those without. Webb and Sieve in a fresh analysis of the data for 1964 separate out families with one from those with both parents earning. They suggest that most of this apparent bias in favour of children is due to the fact that in families with dependent children the mother is likely to be employed. As regards benefits, Nicholson finds that benefits are progressive, representing a higher proportion of the income of those with lower incomes. It does however seem inappropriate to assess the redistributive effects of benefits on this basis. The more significant question is whether those on a lower income receive a higher absolute amount of benefits compared with the rich.

In considering the series as a whole, Webb and Sieve conclude:[27]

> We are now in a position to answer the questions we asked earlier about the role of social policy in producing greater inequality [sic]. To judge from Nicholson's findings the answer must be largely a negative one, for neither pre- nor post-redistribution incomes have become substantially more equal since before the war. At any one time welfare policies seem to be effective in reducing inequality; but the major post-war changes, which have been so widely assumed to be beneficent and equalitarian, have made no difference to estimates of inequality.

Redistribution over time

Essentially, as has been indicated in the discussion of redistribution over the lifespan, redistribution over time is a question of levels of investment. This may be in capital goods (in the social services primarily in buildings) or in people, especially through education and training.

Often decisions about redistribution over time appear as a choice between quality and quantity. Given limited resources for house-building it is possible to use them to produce many cheap houses whose standards will be inadequate in thirty years' time, or fewer houses of a quality that will meet the standards of the next generation. Similarly it is often possible to produce an immediate increase in the output of workers to perform a particular function at the expense of the quality of training. The consequences of this are likely to be more serious in the long run than in the short run.

Most major reorganisations such as the creation of the Social Services Departments in 1971, and the subsequent reorganisation of local government and the health services, result in an immediate deterioration in current services in the interests of future improvement.

Geographical redistribution

If the most important aim of the social services is to relate needs and resources, it is clearly unsatisfactory if the chances of people receiving a service varies according to where they live. The aim of equalising provision between geographical areas has been termed by Bleddyn Davies 'territorial justice'.[28]

The relative quality of social service provision in different areas is strongly influenced by historical factors and particularly the changing geographical patterns of economic development, and the movements of population associated with this. Declining areas tend to lose the younger members of the population of working age, especially those with skills and initiative, leaving behind the elderly and the less able. The environment is particularly unsatisfactory. Housing, schools, hospitals and other buildings have been built to the standards of a previous generation and often poorly maintained. The financial resources needed to rectify this situation are also reduced by the low income from industry and employment. The poor environment also discourages the recruitment of well qualified staff into the social services. This process can take place on a relatively large regional scale as in the industrial areas of north-east and north-west England, and the rural areas of Scotland, Wales, Ireland and Cornwall. It can also take place on a smaller scale in the 'down-town' areas of cities and towns, whether the latter are prosperous or not.

The converse of this is the effect of the influx of population into a prosperous area with the consequent pressure on capital resources such as houses and schools. Since the new immigrants are likely to concentrate in the poorer districts of the area into which they have come this further intensifies existing geographical problems. However, this is basically a much healthier position than that of declining areas, at least in the longer term.

The pervading influence of history on relative levels of social service provision is indicated by Davies's conclusion

73

that the best predictor of the number of places in homes for the elderly in local authority areas in 1948 was population distribution and the willingness of Poor Law authorities to spend a hundred years earlier. Similarly the number of places in 1948 was the best predictor of the number of places provided in 1964.[29]

One way of meeting these disparities is to concentrate responsibility for social services on central government, which can apportion costs according to ability to pay and distribute resources according to need. This was the solution adopted for the social security system, but it is relatively rare in the British social services. The National Health Service is the only other major example in which the distribution of costs was an important consideration in determining its national basis. Both services have made enormous improvements in territorial justice as compared with the situation before the Second World War. In social security major disparities have been largely limited to a minority of discretionary benefits, and even then differences in treatment may be due as much to personal idiosyncrasies as to historical and geographical factors. In the health service the problem has been more intractable. General practitioner services, though fully financed by central government, are provided under a contractual arrangement that retains the professional independence of the practitioners. Distribution can be influenced but not controlled by government, and there are still areas with a long-standing shortage of general practitioners and dentists.[30] There is also some evidence of a poorer quality of service in certain deprived areas.[31] Similar disparities exist in the hospital service based partly on problems of the mobility of staff, and partly on the distribution of old hospital buildings, medical schools and certain traditional attitudes to the practice of medicine in different areas.[32]

Most social services are provided through local authorities which have a large measure of autonomy and raise part of their financial resources locally. In these services quite extreme disparities have persisted. Some of these disparities exist because of deliberate policy decisions of the elected councils to restrict some or all forms of expenditure. Davies[33] and Boaden[34] have both found that the level of expenditure on services tends to be higher if the Labour Party is in power in an authority as opposed to the Conservative Party. The extent to which the central government uses its power and authority to control such policy decisions is discussed in a later chapter. The main concern of this chapter is the efforts of central government to ensure a fair distribution of resources between local authorities, so that the desire to achieve good standards is not blocked by local deprivation.

There are two broad approaches to redistribution between local authorities. The first is positive and involves the provision of resources by central government to the poorer local authorities. The second approach is negative involving the rationing of scarce resources so that too large a share does not go to the more fortunate and prosperous areas.

The positive approach to distribution is primarily applicable to correcting the unequal distribution of financial resources.

Until the Local Government Act of 1929 no attempt was made to relate the distribution of grants from central government to the means of local authorities except in the field of education.[35] The most typical form of grant was a variable grant based either on a percentage of expenditure on a particular service, or on units of service provision such as the number of houses built or persons assisted. Under this system the poorest authorities would be likely to receive less support than wealthier authorities just because of the problem of finding the money for the initial outlay. From 1929 onwards, in successive Local Government Acts in 1929, 1948, 1958 and 1966 increasing importance has been attached to the means of individual local authorities in determining their share of central government grants.

Under the Local Government Act 1966 the distribution of Rate Support Grant from central government for each local authority is based on three elements—a needs element, a resources element and a domestic element. The needs element is based mainly on the total population of the local authority area and the number of children under fifteen. In addition, but to a lesser degree certain other factors are taken into account such as the number of people over sixty-five, high population density, road mileage in relation to population and a declining population. The resources element brings up to an average standard of income areas with a low rateable value in relation to the size of their population. The domestic element is designed to counteract the regressive effect of the rating system by transferring part of the rates that would fall on domestic housing to the central exchequer. This element is concerned with individual rather than territorial justice.

The resources element seems to have been reasonably successful in counteracting the effects of low rateable value on expenditure on services. Both Davies[36] and Boaden[37] in their studies of differences of expenditure between county boroughs, concluded that there is little relationship between the rateable value of property in local authority areas and expenditure on services.

The needs element remains extremely crude. It takes in very few of the criteria suggested earlier as indicating the need for geographical redistribution. It is true that a poor environment would be reflected in the low rateable value that is the basis for the resources element of the grant. But this is only used to bring income up to an average standard, and not to raise income to a level which will overcome the environmental deficiencies.

There are two major problems in improving the sensitivity of the needs element in the grants. First, there are the political problems of getting the local authorities to agree to the use of a system that will inevitably favour the minority of poor authorities to the possible detriment of a much wider number of more prosperous areas. Second, and related to this, is devising indices which can be seen to be objective and fair.[38] The information on which the indices are based should not normally be collected by the authorities themselves because of the danger of manipulating statistics. In the present needs index the most important statistics concern population and are collected by the Registrar-General. Neither should the index encourage the neglect of services by giving higher grants to those whose failure to make adequate provision in the past has significantly contributed to their current high level of need. This, of course, is another example of the incentive problem. Amos, for example, in the City of Liverpool, has devised a social malaise index which could provide the basis for differential provision in different wards of the city.[39] But this index could not be used as the basis for distribution between different authorities as many of the statistics on which the index is based are dependent on local authority activity. For example he found that among the significant indicators of social malaise were the statistics for children deloused, welfare conference cases, and various forms of crime all of which can be influenced by levels of activity.

Davies has discussed some of the problems of constructing indices of need for the purposes of comparing the standards of provision for old people and children in different local authorities.[40] For services for old people he constructed two indices of need; the Family Care Index which took into account the age structure and marital status of the elderly population; and the Social Care Index which took into account housing conditions, housing scarcity, poverty and morbidity. In his analysis of services, however, he had to omit certain county boroughs, which were seaside resorts, spas or administrative centres, because their social structure differed too greatly from other county boroughs and doubt was thrown on the validity of their positions on the indices. Davies's work, though designed for a purpose rather different from the allocation of grants, at least suggests that it would be possible to devise indices that would be more sensitive to need than the present system. Whether their nature and objectivity could be made sufficiently clear to be acceptable to local authorities is a different matter.

Meanwhile some tentative attacks on the problems of deprived areas have been made through various *ad hoc* schemes directed mainly at the inner city areas of the larger metropolises. These schemes include the urban aid programme, the education priority areas and the Home Office community development programme.[41] The *ad hoc* nature of these schemes is generally justified on the grounds of their experimental nature. They do have the advantage of encouraging local initiative and a flexible approach. But their scale is not large enough for the size of the problems that are at issue, and the selection of the areas that receive extra resources is inevitably relatively arbitrary. The problem is very like that of defining the boundaries of the 'development areas' which received special help to encourage the development of new industries. Immediately round the boundaries were many areas whose position was little if any better than the designated areas.[42]

The position of these 'grey' areas was often adversely affected by the special treatment accorded to their neighbours. Hatch and Sherrott found a similar continuum of deprivations in the wards of two inner city areas and concluded that 'any index that attempts to summarise a wide range of deprivations will not be very effective or precise in identifying areas'.[43]

The negative approach to territorial justice, the rationing of scarce resources, has been primarily applied to the control of capital projects, and to a much lesser extent to the control of scarce personnel.

Local authority capital investment represents a significant proportion of national investment. So the total local authority investment programme has to be controlled in the interests of the management of the economy as a whole. If such projects are financed out of current revenue, no problem arises. But if local authorities finance them out of loans, as they usually do, they can contribute to inflation. So the central government sets limits on the loans that it will sanction for local authorities.[44]

Control of capital projects, like the distribution of grants, can be used as a means of influencing policy as well as the distribution of resources. Indeed Griffith in his study of the relations between central departments and local authorities, indicates that approval of capital projects is given first on the issues of policy, and only after that is the question of the effect on total investment considered.[45] Central control of course only influences distribution if total demand does exceed the limit set by the government. Griffith contrasts the position with regard to house-building and school-building in the period which he was describing.[46] In the approval of housing plans, the Ministry of Housing and Local Government had been able to avoid the difficulties of selection and rejection, largely because apathetic authorities failed to submit programmes and the Ministry did not consider that it had any responsibility for pressing them to do so. On the other hand requests for approval for school-building always exceeded the total that could be approved. However even in school-building the primary consideration in accepting or rejecting proposals, was meeting the basic need of enough school places for the relevant population. Only a relatively small proportion of the total could be allocated to take into account needs due to decaying buildings and a substandard environment. Thus most new building was directed into areas of expanding population not the declining inner city areas.

Direction of skilled personnel into areas of special need is not used in Britain in peacetime, although civil servants may be subjected to geographical transfers, at least if they want promotion. Occasionally positive inducements are given to encourage movement into deprived areas, as in special payments to teachers in the educational priority areas, and to general practitioners entering 'under-doctored' areas. The negative approach of quotas has been used in the local authority system for distributing newly qualified teachers,[47] and in the National Health Service by preventing general practitioners from moving into 'over-doctored' areas.[48] In the Probation and After-Care Service a similar effect is intended through central control of the establishment of local services.[49]

Rationing

The controls described above are examples of 'rationing'. In the economic market it is one of the functions of price to ration goods by equating supply with economic demand. So in a free market if the demand for loans by local authorities at a certain level of interest exceeded the money available for this purpose, the interest rate would rise, discouraging some, and probably the poorer authorities from borrowing and at the same time persuading more people to consider lending to local authorities. Similarly competition for teachers among local authorities would result either in an increase in the salaries paid by some authorities, or the movement of teachers to those authorities that offered the best facilities or the best social environment to the detriment of deprived areas.

Within the welfare system in general, services are provided to consumers either free or at a heavily subsidised cost, so that rationing by price no longer takes place. The central rationing problem of distributing scarce resources between competing claimants remains.

Parker[50] has pointed out how in this situation rationing often takes place unconsciously through the use of irrational methods. He describes five such methods.

The method of deterrence is particularly associated with the Poor Law, which was based in the nineteenth century on the principle of deterrence. Overt use of the principle is much less common now, but it still occurs in many subtler forms through the manner in which a service is administered.

Another rationing procedure is to have arbitrary conditions of eligibility. Child guidance clinics run by education authorities will often not treat adolescents who have left school. Housing departments may use long residential qualification as a means of reducing the demand for housing.

Delay is a third method of rationing, usually evidenced by a waiting list or queue. The existence of a waiting list or queue deters some claimants from even applying for help; others may have found some other solution or just given up by the time their turn comes.

Misunderstanding and the failure to dispel ignorance are particularly common. Numerous surveys have shown the extent of ignorance about the existence of benefits and how even those who know of them may fail to realise that they themselves are eligible. Few social services are effectively advertised.

Finally Parker suggests that services may be rationed by dilution—by reducing the standards of the service provided. More clients may be seen but their problems given less attention; more students may be taken on courses but the quality of the education reduced by failure to expand staff and material facilities. This may often be the most appropriate form of rationing. If the dilution is even, it may also be fair. It has one great advantage over all other forms of rationing, including rationing by price, that the level of potential demand is much more accurately known. On the other hand it may result in spreading the resources so thinly that no one benefits; if it is unconscious many of the effects may go unrecognised; and it is likely to result in failure to make a proper decision about priorities.

The effect of these methods of rationing is to produce an arbitrary distribution of scarce resources, which is in some respects little better and in other respects worse than that produced by a laissez-faire economic market. Even rational methods of rationing by means other than price are likely to have one significant side-effect. This is to produce a double system of provision. The second system rises beside the rationed service and enables people to get a better or a quicker service for a price. Frequently this price will be a higher one than would naturally occur through the unfettered operation of the economic market. An example of this is the effect of planning procedures on the price of land with planning permission. Another example is the way in which some specialists encourage National Health Service patients waiting for treatment to 'jump the queue' by offering it for a fee through private practice. If rationing is tight and there is no legal market alternative, this can result in illegal activities or a 'black market'.

Economic appraisal

A major advantage of the economic market as a means of rationing resources is that it uses a single unit of measure for the evaluation of numerous and varied items. This makes possible a comparison of the results of alternative courses of action involving the use of different resources for the same or different products. If similar procedures can be used to evaluate public services they could be a great aid to the determination of priorities.

It is important to remember, as was pointed out in the first chapter, that this type of economic appraisal is simplified for commercial concerns by their autonomy. They can ignore externalities and the loss of service by customers who cannot afford to pay. The measurement of most costs is externally determined, and the value of the product, while subject to uncertainty, is also controlled by external factors, that eventually make possible an objective determination. Profit is generally an adequate criterion of success. For the state these simplifications are often either not available, or not permissible. One of the functions of the welfare system is to take account of the externalities of the economic market including costs and benefits which are not evaluated in the economic market. Providing services without charge or at a highly sub-sidised price, the state is deprived of an 'objective' evaluation of its services. Profit is unacceptable as a substitute for the social evaluation of the results of activities.

The most popular term for the economic appraisal of state provision is 'cost-benefit analysis'. Originally this was used for the appraisal of investment policies and there is some advantage in limiting it to this type of decision. Peters[51] describes the procedures as follows:

1 Define the project with a list of the current benefits and costs.
2 The list of benefits and costs, direct and indirect, must be reduced to monetary values in order to arrive at an estimate of the current net benefit of the project (if any).
3 Compare the stream of annual net benefits with the capital cost of the project.

In its simplest terms the annual value, after an allow-ance has been made for the net depreciation of capital assets, might be expressed as a percentage rate of return on capital.

A decision must then be made on whether the rate of return is high enough compared with alternative forms of invest-ment.

Each of these stages involves major methodological problems which limit the value of the conclusions. The advantages and limitations of the method are well illustrated by the argument in *New Society* between Hall and Self on the Report on the Third London Airport.[52] Self takes the view that the whole exercise gives a spurious objectivity to decisions that must ultimately be taken on political grounds. Hall believes that this form of analysis provides the best evidence on which such political decisions can be taken. Essentially the issue is the weight that should be attached to the analysis when the final decisions are made.

Cost-benefit analysis was first applied to large-scale invest-ment decisions such as hydro-electric and transport schemes.[53] The purpose of such schemes is primarily economic, so that many of the major costs and benefits are readily evaluated in economic terms. The evaluation of social costs and benefits is a secondary refinement. Similar analyses have since been applied to broad education and health programmes.[54] Education again has important economic objectives, and many of its benefits are directly reflected in the wages and salaries paid in the economic market. It is not unreasonable to assume that the marginal increase in salaries that results from the possession of educational qualifications gives a broad indication of the value placed on these by society.[55] But in the field of health an economic return from rehabilitation or the prevention of an early death can only be expected in a limited number of cases generally within a limited age range. A reduction of infant mortality or the prolongation of the lives of the elderly may represent a negative economic benefit to society. The grounds for action are moral and the benefits cannot be evaluated in economic terms. There is even less room for the economic appraisal of benefits when one comes to the evaluation of services such as the social care of children and of the mentally handicapped.

Where the aims of services are primarily social rather than economic a rather different form of economic appraisal becomes desirable. This is cost-effectiveness analysis, or—a broader concept—cost-effect analysis.[56] The first essential of this type of appraisal is cost analysis. This is a form of accounting that is normal practice in commercial enterprises but rare in public service, under which all the costs of production are allocated to the products to which they directly contribute. For example in estimating the cost of hospital treatment for a particular type of case, account would be taken of the cost of the time devoted to an average case by different types of staff, the cost of food, its preparation and service, and an appropriate proportion of the overheads, including the capital costs of the hospital. To do this there has to be an initial investigation into the way in which time and other resources are allocated by staff to the care of different patients. Such an investigation is expensive but it does make possible a comparison between the real costs of different forms of care. It also often leads to a more efficient use of scarce resources by pinpointing wasteful activities, and those in which skilled personnel are used for unskilled tasks.

Once the costing has been done, the effectiveness of different forms of treatment or care can be examined, and the contribution of additional resources to the quality of care assessed. For example the paraplegic study described in the next chapter[57] recommended that consideration should be given to holding case conferences at the time of discharge of patients and about three months later. The cost analysis of a case conference would probably reveal that it was very expensive. If the improvement in the care of patients resulting from this proved to be small, the time of the people involved would probably be better used for some other purpose, and some less expensive improvement in communication tested.

Cost-effectiveness analysis focuses on the particular results aimed at by the services provided, e.g. the rehabilitation of a particular patient. Cost-effect analysis recognises that the provision of services in particular ways may produce results, good and bad, other than those intended. Thus the arrangement of case conferences for a small number of conditions presenting particular difficulties might have additional results in improving communication about other cases. An increase in family care for the elderly might improve the condition of the elderly people concerned, but result in the physical or psychological deterioration of other members of the families. Such benefits or costs are a form of externality that should be taken into account in the analysis, if this is possible.

Chapter 5
Co-ordination

Summary of the argument

Co-ordination is defined as institutionalised co-operation—that is co-operation systematised by defining roles and by developing procedures for the avoidance of conflicting decisions and for joint planning. It may also be concerned with the consistency of parallel decisions.

Communication is both a prerequisite and an aim of co-ordination. Systems of communication may be hampered by mechanical problems, which can often only be overcome by redundancy in communication; by problems of language, particularly professional jargons; and by the effects of hierarchy on communication upwards through an organisation. On the other hand the existence of hierarchy is often essential for effective decision-making between different individuals, different occupations and different organisations. The specialisation of social service organisations on the basis of skills tends to institutionalise conflicts of values in opposing hierarchies, with an inadequate system of arbitration in the interests of consistent action. The resultant problems of co-ordination are intensified by the failure of social-service agencies to take account of externalities of cost.

Co-ordination takes place at different administrative levels in the state, at national, regional, local, local community and consumer levels. At lower levels the major task is the co-ordination of consumption, that is the development of precisely planned programmes that will meet the particular needs of the consumer and take into account the idiosyncratic capacities of individual workers. At higher levels the primary task is the co-ordination of provision, that is ensuring that adequate facilities without excess provision or gaps, are available from which a choice can be made to meet the needs of the consumer. Measures to improve co-ordination of either consumption or provision will not necessarily improve co-ordination of the other.

Effective delegation of decision-making is generally necessary to ensure co-ordination of consumption. This makes it more difficult to ensure consistency of standards.

Co-ordination and co-operation

Co-ordination is a word that is used frequently without any discussion of its meaning. Slack[1] has emphasised the difference between co-ordination and co-operation. This is another example of related terms which may be used in different senses by different writers. Slack attempts to make a clear distinction between them by suggesting that co-operation takes place between individuals, and co-ordination between services. There seems little justification for these definitions. It seems perfectly acceptable to describe as co-ordination the planning of interdependent activities by two individuals, or to describe as co-operation work performed jointly by two institutions.

In its derivation, co-operation appears to be the generic term for working together. Co-ordination implies planning and can be regarded as institutionalised co-operation—co-operation is systematised by defining roles and by developing procedures for the avoidance of conflicting decisions and for joint planning. Because the systematic planning of joint activities involves a commitment from all parties to the final plan, co-ordination usually includes an element of obligation, which may be enforced by sanctions. If co-ordination is given this meaning it will be convenient to confine the use of the term co-opera-tion to joint activities of an *ad hoc* or voluntary nature. In these senses both terms can be applied to individuals and to organisations, although the latter because of the complexity of their work and their need for consistency, are more likely to engage in co-ordinated rather than co-operative activities.

In one sense however, co-ordination may go beyond the concept of co-operation. It is concerned also with the cohesive-ness of decisions and activities that only indirectly affect one another, for example the consistency of parallel decisions in different cases.

Effective communication is both a prerequisite and an aim

of co-ordination. It is a prerequisite in that co-ordination cannot take place unless those who make interrelated decisions can communicate with each other and those who are to carry out the decisions know what is required of them. It is an aim of co-ordination in that systematic planning is usually required to ensure that communication takes place.

There are many kinds of problem in developing effective systems of communication. Three of these deserve mention here—problems of mechanics, problems of language and problems created by the existence of hierarchies.

Mechanical problems concern the means of communication. For co-ordinated activity to take place it is necessary to ensure that information is given at the right time to everyone who needs it, that it is understood, and that it is remembered when it is required for action. The two main methods are oral and written communication which have complementary advantages and disadvantages. Oral communication can generally be made to command attention, but only from those present when it is given; written communications can more easily be circulated to everyone, but there is little guarantee that everyone will read them. In oral communication there can be feedback about problems of comprehension and action—which is less possible through the written word—but there is no easy way of refreshing the memory or correcting conflicting memories of what has been said. The written document is definitive, or if ambiguous at least the source of the ambiguity can be traced. It can also be used to refresh the memory—if it is not lost. Oral communication is often particularly expensive of time; written documents present a problem of filing, and destruction of the obsolete. Because no method of communication is foolproof effective systems normally require a good deal of redundancy, combining both oral and written elements.

Language barriers are obviously of considerable importance in preventing effective communication. In the co-ordination of the social services major barriers are created by the occupational jargons peculiar to different professional groups. Professional jargons generally include a great many technical terms which increase the precision of communication within the profession and with others familiar with the jargon. But such jargons also often have secondary functions concerned with the maintenance of the unity and exclusiveness of the occupational group. Correct use of the jargon helps to distinguish the initiates of the profession and to give them a sense of common identity. It also emphasises the esoteric nature of professional knowledge on which the power and authority of the profession generally rests. So an intrinsic problem of communicating technical information to the layman is likely to be complicated by a reluctance to make information comprehensible.

The use of a technical jargon is likely to complicate another language problem which may affect the outcome of co-ordinated action if not co-ordination itself. This is the problem of communication between middle-class officials or professionals and working-class clients, described by Bernstein. This has been discussed particularly in relation to teachers[2] and social workers.[3]

The effect of mechanical and language problems on co-ordination is well illustrated by a casestudy of the aftercare of paraplegic patients.[4]

Paraplegia is a condition of partial or complete paralysis due to injury or disease of the spinal cord. The rehabilitation of paraplegics requires a combination of varied skills and services in the hospital and community, so co-ordination is important. It is a relatively rare condition, so that full use of hospital facilities requires a wide catchment area, while most social service personnel including general practitioners are unlikely to be familiar with the condition and its treatment.

The study in question was based on a centre at Southport that drew its cases from the whole of the north-west region and beyond. Because of the wide catchment area it was impossible for the hospital staff to know well either the personnel or the systems employed by the numerous local authorities and other agencies with which they had contact. Distance also often made face-to-face contact difficult. Ten patients were selected for study who had been recently discharged to two hospitals and five local authority areas. Communications were explored by interviewing the patients and their relatives, the general practitioners and the local authority staff involved in each case.

Within the hospital the consultant was leader and co-ordinator of a small team of personnel with complementary skills and functions. Regular face-to-face contact in situations in which there was a free interchange of information meant that communication presented few problems. Within the community services the consultant saw the general practitioner as performing a similar role. Thus it seemed reasonable to him that his only direct communication with the community services was through the general practitioner. The procedure adopted was to send a formal notification when the patient was admitted to the centre, and then at the time of his discharge to send a detailed account of his medical condition. To avoid infringing the general practitioner's prerogatives, no instructions were given about treatment except perhaps to recommend the continuation of physiotherapy or similar treatment, and it was left to the general practitioner to get in touch with the consultant if he needed further advice.

Because the consultant saw the general practitioner as the main co-ordinator of the services for the patient, his communications with the local authorities were left to the medical social worker, and were largely limited to requests for home nursing equipment, and, where appropriate, housing adaptations or rehousing. After discussing the home situation with the patient and his relative, the medical social worker wrote to the medical officer of health of the appropriate authority requesting help with these items. These requests were then passed by the medical officer of health to the appropriate officer or department. For example, the request for home nursing equipment, which is required in every case, was passed to the district nurse through the district nurse supervisor.

The analysis of this system and its effects revealed a number of weaknesses. First of all, communication between the centre and the community services was almost entirely one way with no feedback except where the district nurses took the initiative in contacting the centre. Since the information to be conveyed was complex and involved the community workers learning about an unfamiliar situation, difficulties inevitably arose. Moreover, the consultant and other staff at the centre were unlikely to receive information on the effectiveness of the arrangements they had made.

Second, these difficulties were increased by the way in which specialist information was filtered through people without knowledge of the specialist skills and jargons. Thus because the information received by the medical officer of health came through the medical social worker, he tended to lack precise information about the medical condition of the patient, and this affected what he passed on to the housing and other departments. Similarly information from the occupational and physiotherapists' departments in the paraplegic centre was passed through two doctors, the consultant and the general practitioner, before it reached the therapists in the local hospitals. All detailed assessment had by this time been removed.

Third, the consultant's picture of the role of the general practitioner as a co-ordinator proved completely false. Some co-ordination was provided by the medical officer of health, but he had no direct contact with the patient and little with the centre. Moreover, the medical officer of health received a letter related to specific needs of the patient and responded accordingly. For instance, although the medical officers of health believed that paraplegics were likely to need casework help, no referral was made to the welfare department unless home adaptation or rehousing was required. Similarly, welfare officers who visited in connection with these needs did not necessarily follow up to see whether casework help was needed. In fact within the local authorities, a concept of the role of the general practitioner was held similar to that of the consultant. So no member of the local authority staff attempted to make a total assessment of the needs of the patient and his family. Since the general practitioner made very few requests for help with services, the services that were received by the patients and their families depended on the initiative shown by field staff, who were not necessarily clear about their responsibilities in this respect.

Hierarchy and communication

The existence of a hierarchical structure may aid the transmission of information down an organisation but there is a good deal of evidence from empirical and field studies that it inhibits communication from lower to higher levels.[5] The authority of the superior tends to produce a reluctance to contradict him and gives an undue weight to his views. The greater his power, in the form of control over rewards and punishments, the greater reluctance there will be to pass on information that will displease him even if the information is not to the detriment of the informer. As a result it is often difficult for those at higher levels in the hierarchy to know what is really happening. This is of particular significance in the social services where most of those in direct contact with clients or patients, who therefore have most knowledge of their needs, are relatively low in the hierarchy. Similar problems arise where there is a hierarchy of professions, and interprofessional co-operation is required.

In part at least this difficulty can be overcome by adopting an appropriate style of leadership, and here there is a tendency for the style of leadership accepted at the top of a hierarchical organisation to affect all lower levels. For example Revans[6] undertook a comparative study of the efficiency of hospitals, defining efficiency in terms of the length of time patients remained in hospital for similar conditions, and staff turnover. Focusing on ward sisters as key figures in the running of hospitals he found that both criteria of efficiency were highly correlated with the attitudes of the ward sisters to their superiors and to student nurses. Where the ward sisters felt there was a lack of interest, respect and support for their work from matrons, consultants and other staff, they gave less weight to teaching and supporting the student nurses. Where these negative attitudes occurred, staff turnover was naturally higher, but also patients remained longer in hospital. This latter result Revans attributed to the failure of communication that occurred in this situation. Significantly efficiency was not related to the importance attached by ward sisters to the outward manifestations of hierarchical status, like separate dining facilities.

Hierarchy and co-ordination

While it is perfectly possible for a great deal of co-ordination to take place on the basis of discussion between equals there is a good deal of evidence that a hierarchical structure can be very important in speeding up decision-making or even making decisions possible. Blau and Scott,[7] after a careful analysis of the evidence, suggests that there is a clear distinction in this respect between problem-solving and co-ordination. In problem-solving a free flow of information ensures the consideration of all relevant ideas. This free flow is assisted by the absence of hierarchy. On the other hand to obtain co-ordination, the flow of discussion has to be cut to ensure a focus on the most fruitful alternatives and eventually to decide on a particular course of action.

Even where there is no conflict of interest, the existence of hierarchy even on an informal basis, can ensure that a decision is taken between rival proposals more quickly, and therefore in many cases more effectively. If there are also conflicting interests involved, then a hierarchical structure is likely to be essential to ensure that a decision is taken without a damaging power struggle.

Stevenson[8] examined the conflicts that underlie some problems of co-ordination between social workers and welfare workers from different agencies helping the same families. She grouped these under several headings. First, there were problems of philosophy—ideas about the ultimate aims of the social services which were themselves related to views about the nature of man and how men should be treated. Second, there were disagreements about the relevance of different casework skills. This can be generalised to all social services if one enlarges it to a consideration of skills and methods other than social work, such as educational, medical and administrative skills. Third, Stevenson discerned conflicts of function and involvement. Because different social services have different functions, their workers are likely to identify more strongly with the needs of different people involved in the situation. Thus a social worker may tend to identify with a deprived family; an official of the housing department, considering the same family, may feel more strongly about the needs of his more 'normal' tenants or 'more deserving' people on the waiting list; an officer of the supplementary benefits commission may be particularly concerned about protecting the public purse, and therefore taxpayers, from abuse.

It is of course entirely proper that these conflicting views should be expressed and considered in the problem-solving process. This can best be achieved in a situation of equality between the representatives of the services. But equally there is a need for consistency of action which is only likely to be achieved within the context of hierarchy.

The social services are organised into systems based on particular functions that are themselves often delineated in relation to particular occupational skills. One effect of this is to assist each system to develop a consensus on the values, skills and objectives relevant to its function. This consensus is partly dictated by the function itself, partly by the selection of workers entering the system, and the socialisation process they undergo in training before or after entry. But above all it is reinforced by a hierarchical structure, often based on a particular occupational group such as doctors, teachers or social workers, which suppresses conflicting opinions in a variety of ways. Commitment to the system is further ensured by the way in which the status and power of individuals and occupational groups depends on the maintenance of the system.

The consequences of the commitment of personnel to the particular functions of a department or agency was raised by Stevenson.[9] She pointed out that the identification with particular functions is often useful at lower levels in the administration, because it helps the worker to focus his work. But at higher levels it can be very damaging because conflict becomes institutionalised in opposing hierarchies and there may be no effective system for arbitration at any level.

The problems of co-ordination created by differences in the criteria for decisions adopted by different organisations is often intensified by the reluctance to take account of externalities created by their decisions, where the costs of a decision fall on another department or agency. A classic example of this is the way in which at one time local authority housing departments would evict families in arrears in rent, who would then go into temporary accommodation provided by the welfare departments under the National Assistance Act.[10] The welfare departments in turn would evict the families from this accommodation at the end of a specified period, with the result that the children were taken into care. At each stage the weekly cost to the local authority became substantially greater. Another example is the failure of local authorities to provide adequate services for the elderly, the mentally ill and the mentally subnormal in the community so that people occupy expensive, and often unsuitable hospital accommodation because they cannot be discharged.[11] Similarly hospitals have tended to redefine their role as curative and refuse to accept responsibility for care of many conditions without considering the implications for other services and for the patients and their families.[12] It is one of the advantages of cost-effect and cost-benefit analyses that they can be used across the boundaries of services, so that they can take account of such externalities.[13]

Dimensions and levels of co-ordination

Rodgers[14] has distinguished three dimensions and five levels of co-ordination.

The three dimensions of co-ordination that she puts forward are vertical, between different hierarchical levels within organisations and systems, horizontal, between individuals and organisations at the same level, and over time. The latter she puts forward tentatively in connection with the need for continuity in the relationship between social workers and their clients, but it obviously has a much wider importance than this. Consistency of decisions over time is essential both to ensure justice to individuals and effectiveness in action. The problems of vertical and horizontal co-ordination have been discussed in the previous section.

Rodgers's five levels of co-ordination are national, regional, local, local community and consumer. To some extent this choice of levels is arbitrary, although Rodgers is able to make effective use of it in considering the services in four countries with quite different circumstances, Britain, France, Norway and Canada. A closer examination of these levels suggests that different processes are involved at the lower levels as compared with the higher levels.

For the people who are consumers of the services, particularly individuals and families, there is a need for a precisely planned programme which ensures that the right mixture of services is available at the right time. This was clearly the problem in the paraplegic study quoted earlier. At higher levels co-ordination is much more concerned with ensuring that enough of the different services are available to meet the total needs of the area concerned rather than the co-ordination of specific activities. These two processes may be called the co-ordination of consumption and the co-ordination of provision respectively. A useful comparison is provided by the roles of the shopkeeper and the housewife working on a tight budget. It is the shopkeeper's responsibility to provide an appropriate range of goods on his shelves; it is the housewife's responsibility to select the particular goods that will meet the needs of her family over a particular period and for specific meals. Obviously these processes have many similarities; the difference lies in the precision of timing and communication required to ensure the interlocking of activities at the consumption level.

The co-ordination of provision and of consumption are of course closely connected processes. There is a need for vertical co-ordination between the two, particularly to avoid waste of resources and gaps in provision. But they are also to some extent independent of one another, in the sense that improvement in one will not necessarily result in improvement in the other. If co-ordination of provision is defective, this will limit the choices open at the consumption level but will not abrogate the need for effective procedures at that level to make the best use of what resources are provided. Similarly, however good the co-ordination of provision, poor co-ordination at the consumption level will mean a poor service to the consumer. Thus there is no reason to think that a reorganisation of the health service designed to meet the criticisms levelled at the effects of the tripartite structure on health service provision will necessarily have any effect on the sort of problems revealed by the paraplegic study described earlier.

Relating this dual division to Rodgers's levels of administration, it is clear that the higher one goes the less important is the co-ordination of consumption as a function of administration, but it may still appear even at a national level, if the scale of the service warrants it. The prison system or the preparations made for the care of Asian immigrants from Uganda in

1972 are examples. But in general most co-ordination that relates to consumption patterns occurs in the local community, or in helping individuals and families.

Delegation and co-ordination

To provide effective co-ordination at the level of consumption requires considerable flexibility. Not only is the situation of each client or client system[15] often unique in the particular combination of needs that it presents, but different workers from the same profession also vary in the contribution that they can make to helping their clients. While there may be some uniformity in their basic skills, they have differences in expertise and even greater differences in personality and attitudes which enable them to give some types of assistance but not others. Some district nurses may have the personal qualities and interests which enable them to provide assistance which in other cases might more appropriately be given by social workers; some social workers may have particular experience of health problems or even training as a nurse which might enable them to give advice which another worker would refer to a health visitor. This makes it much less justifiable, and in some cases impossible to define roles precisely according to the professional training of the worker. The individual planning for clients should thus take into account the idiosyncrasies of the workers as well as of the clients and their situation.

Flexibility of this degree requires the delegation of responsibility for decision-making to a very low level in the hierarchical structure of social service organisations preferably to the front-line workers. This is particularly necessary if the workers who must co-operate come from different organisations.

Delegation of responsibility to front-line workers in order to ensure a flexible response to individual need makes it much more difficult to ensure uniformity of standards and a consistent policy from one case to another. So flexibility may result in apparent or actual injustice. Decisions may seem unjust because the criteria, though correctly applied, are not clear to outside observers. They may actually be unjust because policy is wrongly interpreted as a result of error or bias in the decision-maker. This is one of the basic dilemmas in the administration of social services.

This problem is well illustrated by the dilemma of discretion in the administration of supplementary benefits. The need for discretion is justified by the importance of flexibility in meeting individual need. It is opposed by those who believe that justice will be achieved more effectively if benefits are given of right and the rules are widely known and freely available. Hence the pressure to publish the 'A' code, the system of secret rules by which the decisions of officers of the Supplementary Benefits Commission are supposed to be determined, publication of which is opposed by the Commission itself. Similar issues are raised by the transfer of responsibility for decisions about juvenile delinquents from courts to social services departments. The carefully regulated powers and procedures of the juvenile courts have been replaced by a much more flexible, but also less open system.

Chapter 6
Power, authority and freedom

Summary of the argument

Power and authority both involve the ability of one person to impose his will on another; power implies that compliance can be obtained by coercion or the manipulation of sanctions and rewards, authority implies legitimacy and acceptability. They can be defined in different ways to make the two concepts mutually exclusive or to varying degrees overlapping. In practice those who have authority tend also to have power, and the authority and power are often derived from similar sources.

The primary sources of authority in our society are the law —rational-legal authority, and knowledge and skills—rational-pragmatic authority. Within the social services dominant hierarchical systems of rational-legal authority like local government and philanthropic organisations are penetrated by other systems based on rational-pragmatic authority.

In our society particular value is attached to 'functional autonomy', the right to make the decisions necessary for the performance of a function without external intervention or supervision. This is one of the dimensions of freedom. A second dimension is presented by the potential for development. At a given level of power there is a tendency for functional autonomy and the potential for development to be inversely correlated. For a system to increase its freedom of action on both dimensions it must increase its level of power.

The development of social services while primarily aimed at the redistribution of resources, has often had a secondary effect on the balance of power. For ideological and practical reasons British governments have been reluctant to increase the power of central government. So the state has tended to use existing institutions, including philanthropic organisations for the provision of social services. This usually results in reinforcing the initial power structure of the institutions in question. Alternatively it has created semi-autonomous bodies such as the regional hospital boards and local authorities to whom it has often given a large measure of functional autonomy despite a high level of financial support.

Differing contractual conditions in providing financial aid affect the degree of functional autonomy of the recipient body.

Power and authority

Power and authority are two concepts which, like income and wealth, have different connotations, yet are very closely allied. Both authority and power involve the ability of one person to impose his will on another without having to convince him first by rational argument. Implicit in the concept of power is the consideration that compliance can be obtained by resort to coercion, by the threat of sanctions or by the manipulation of rewards. Authority implies legitimacy and acceptability.

Weber defined power as 'the probability that one actor within a social relationship will be in a position to carry out his own will despite resistance'.[1] Authority he defined as 'the probability that certain specific commands (or all commands) from a given source will be obeyed by a given group of persons'.[2]

Blau and Scott interpret these definitions as mutually exclusive, the difference lying in the voluntary nature of obedience to authority. However, as they point out this distinction is rarely so clear in practice and Weber's usage is not necessarily followed by others. Most people who have authority in Weber's sense also have power and vice versa, so that it is difficult to know which is relevant in any particular situation. So for some purposes it may be convenient to define authority as a kind of power. Etzioni defines authority as 'legitimate power, that is power that is used in accordance with the subject's values and under conditions that he views as proper'.[3] Warham implicitly takes a similar approach when she defines authority as 'the power to make decisions which determine the conduct of others'.[4] Alternatively power and authority can be seen as overlapping concepts. Legitimate power is only effective if it is also broadly acceptable. So authority may be broadened to include power that is legitimate in society's terms without necessarily being acceptable to the subject of the authority. Other forms of authority may in that case be regarded as distinct from power, just as other forms of power will be seen as distinct from authority. In this book the terms will be treated as mutually exclusive.

Weber distinguishes various sources of power. They include 'physical or psychical compulsion' under the law, sometimes called coercive power, and economic power, stemming from the control of resources.[5] While coercive power has its place in the social services, for example in law enforcement, penal provisions and control of the mentally ill, typically this is confined to control over clients in specific situations and not to workers within the services themselves. Control over resources is generally far more important both for clients and for those who work in the services. Economic power often comes from the ownership or possession of resources—wealth, capital goods, money, skills, or knowledge. Within the social services it frequently derives from a position of authority which gives a person or group who are not themselves owners the right to make decisions about the use of the resources commanded by an organisation. This demonstrates another of the close links between authority and power. Etzioni makes a further distinction between remunerative power, control through material resources, and normative power which depends on the allocation of symbolic rewards like status symbols and marks of esteem and prestige.[6]

Crozier[7] investigating bureaucratic organisations, found that one of the most important sources of power was the control over areas of uncertainty. Control over subordinates is increased by creating areas of uncertainty in which rewards are dependent on maintaining the goodwill of the superordinate. So the subordinate tries to reduce the areas of uncertainty by getting clear rules accepted for all such areas including particularly the conditions for promotion or dismissal. Within the social services the control over uncertainty might well be an important basis for the high prestige and power of the medical and legal professions. In a materialistic world they have largely supplanted the hierarchy of the churches which once exercised power through its claim to control access to the favour of God.

Weber also distinguished three types of authority differentiated by the sources from which they spring.[8] 'Traditional' authority is legitimated by an acceptance of the present social order as inviolable. 'Charismatic' authority depends on the personal qualities of the leader and particularly on belief in the divine nature of his inspiration. 'Legal' authority is legitimated by a belief in the supremacy of law. Institutions in which legal authority predominates are characterised by a system of rules and regulations which provide the basis for decision-making, and a hierarchical structure in which obedience is owed by subordinates to the superordinates subject only to a common obedience to the system of rules. Some writers make an additional distinction between legal authority springing directly from the law, and 'positional' authority deriving from a person's position in the hierarchy.[9] This distinction is useful for some purposes but will not be followed here.

Harrison,[10] in examining power and authority in the Baptist churches in the USA, discerned a fourth type of authority, which he designated 'rational-pragmatic' authority in contrast to Weber's 'rational-legal' type of authority. In the Baptist church legal authority lay with the individual churches, and this authority was theoretically inalienable. In practice certain officials, appointed jointly by the churches, yet given no legal authority, proved particularly influential in the decision-making process, because of the recognition given to their expertise and knowledge. It is clear that this concept of pragmatic authority has wide relevance, since there are many situations in which expertise cuts across the hierarchical structure of organisations—the typical conflict between 'staff' and 'line' in industrial organisations. While rational-legal authority leads to a pyramidical, hierarchic structure, rational-pragmatic authority leads to many centres of authority on a pluralistic model. Control is more evenly distributed and based more clearly on reciprocal relationships.

A clear example of the influence of pragmatic authority can be found in the administrative system of British hospitals.[11] Within the hospitals there are three major parallel systems, the medical staff under the consultants, the nursing staff under the matron, and administrative staff under the hospital secretary.

H

There are also numerous smaller systems such as those of the occupational therapists, medical social workers, and physiotherapists. The consultants are responsible for the care of individual patients, but each consultant is a virtually autonomous centre of authority. Within the limitations imposed by the consultants' responsibility for individual patients, other departments also operate with a large measure of independence.

In our society primacy is increasingly given to 'rational' forms of authority, whether legal or pragmatic. Traditional and charismatic authority, where they have not given way to 'rational' forms of authority, often have to be justified in rational terms. Candidates for most church ministries must generally prove themselves capable of undertaking a course of training as well as showing evidence of 'grace' or vocation. It is now much less easy for people to find a role as 'social workers' merely on the basis of social status or personal qualities as was the case when social work began in the nineteenth century. The traditional authority of the father in a family is now limited by the law much more than it once was and is also probably less likely to be backed by the law where conflict arises. A father must justify his use of authority.

Authority and power tend to arise from the same sources. Within the political system rational-legal authority is legitimated by responsibility to an electorate. The same process of election also legitimates the power of the elected representatives to raise money compulsorily, and to determine the use of resources. Under the elected representatives are hierarchies of paid employees with delegated rational-legal authority, and delegated power.

In the economic system the law sanctions the power given by ownership of money or property. In this case authority seems almost to be a secondary result of the power situation, in that an obedience originally conditioned by the existence of power is accepted as reasonable. Certainly the hierarchies of industry and commerce seem to include elements of power and authority like the hierarchies of government.

The knowledge and skills which form the basis for rational-pragmatic authority, also give power through the ability to give or withhold services—a form of power that is closely related to Crozier's control of areas of uncertainty. The hospital patient may conform to instructions because he believes the medical staff know best or because he believes that if he does not conform he may receive less care. The student may uncritically express a lecturer's known views in an examination, because he respects the lecturer's point of view or because he fears that otherwise he may not pass the examination.

Though rational-pragmatic authority and power are not essentially derived from the law, those with knowledge and skills can increase both their authority and their power by improving their position within the rational-legal system. They may increase their power by gaining a legal monopoly over the performance of certain functions, such as the barrister's right to represent someone before certain courts; by the granting of coercive powers like the right of certain social workers to bring a child before a court; or by gaining a position in a rational-legal hierarchy, like the medical officer of health at the head of a local authority department.

The authority and power that spring from the possession of knowledge and skills are not of course by any means confined to those who are normally regarded as belonging to the professions. Any knowledge that is valued, and limited in its distribution, such as that gained by long experience of a complicated administrative structure, can give both authority and power. The control of information also gives power in relation to both subordinates and superordinates. Thus 'front-line workers',[12] that is workers in direct contact with clients, are generally placed in the lowest levels of the organisational hierarchy. They have power over clients through their control over information and resources that their clients need, and the information that they pass on to those who make decisions; they can also increase their own power in relation to superordinates by restricting the flow of information that makes control over their own activities possible. This same process can be repeated at all levels, hence the importance of channels of communication that by-pass intermediate hierarchical levels.

Those who possess power and authority deriving from a number of different sources can be in a very strong position indeed. Thus the professional worker in charge of a local authority department can have great influence over his committee through his technical expertise, and his control over the information that reaches the committee. The front-line worker who has the expertise and status of a professional like doctors, is likely to be in a strong position to resist control or criticism not only from lay people but also from fellow professionals not in direct contact with the client.

Broadly the social services can be seen as a central series of vertical systems based on rational-legal authority, interpenetrated by other systems based on rational-pragmatic authority. The interpenetration takes place in various ways. People possessing knowledge or skills may gain positions in the hierarchical systems in which their rational-pragmatic authority and power may be reinforced by rational-legal power deriving from their hierarchical status. Or again they may set up their own hierarchical system in rivalry with existing systems. The strategies of interpenetration will be discussed in the next chapter.

Functional autonomy and the parameters of freedom

Comment has already been made on the way in which groups or sub-systems within a larger system attempt to restrict the power of others by developing rules and regulations that limit the areas of uncertainty. The aim of this manœuvre is to achieve an increased measure of what has been termed 'functional autonomy'.[13] Functional autonomy means the right to make the decisions necessary for the performance of a function without external intervention or supervision. Since no part of a system can be totally independent of it while remaining a part, autonomy is always limited. The limits may be wide or narrow, but it is a prerequisite of functional autonomy that whatever limits there are should be clearly defined. Otherwise the existence of uncertainty creates an implicit or explicit external control.

Functional autonomy has values for both the individuals or groups who achieve it and for the system which grants it. To those who achieve it, it gives a sense of freedom which is highly valued in our culture. Gouldner in fact attributed to the search for functional autonomy a major role in creating change within systems which might otherwise tend to a state of equilibrium. For the larger system, granting functional autonomy to its sub-systems simplifies the decision-making process. It avoids the use of controls which can in some cases stultify the objectives they are designed to achieve, by, for example, preventing a flexible response to a changing situation. It may even provide a more effective form of control just because such freedom is desired, and there may be fear of losing it if it is abused.

It can be seen from this discussion that the *laissez-faire* policy pursued by nineteenth-century British governments that left decisions to the working of the economic market and raised to the highest value the independence and self-responsibility of the individual and the family was a policy deliberately designed to maximise functional autonomy. Classical economic theory provided an ideology that helped to legitimate this value system, supporting religious and philosophical attitudes with pseudo-scientific 'laws'. This emphasis on functional autonomy, by contributing to the break up of a system designed for pre-industrial conditions, may have been to some extent a necessary pre-condition of some of the desirable changes that took place in that period.

In chapter 1 it was pointed out that a policy of delegation has a number of disadvantages,[14] and these are equally relevant wherever functional autonomy is granted to an individual or a sub-system. It creates externalities, hinders co-ordination, and makes some desirable objectives unattainable. In fact functional autonomy is only one of the dimensions of freedom. A second dimension is provided by expanding the range of potential achievements. A subsistence farmer may have complete functional autonomy but a low standard of living. If he joins a co-operative he will lose some functional autonomy but will probably increase his standard of living. A general practitioner in a single-handed practice need not defer to anyone in organising his work, but may be on constant call, unable to develop specialist interests and probably have to content himself with poorer supporting facilities. If he enters a group practice he will have to fit in with colleagues in many ways but will be able to improve his position through specialisation and the pooling of resources.

Additional power, and therefore additional freedom in a developmental sense can be gained through control of increased resources. But society will not normally give control over additional resources, except in return for specific services, without at least considering whether further conditions should be attached or further control exercised. The British universities have undergone unprecedented expansion in the years since the Second World War through the injection of government financial support.[15] While their autonomy has remained considerable, they have had to show some willingness to respond to government influence and fears have been expressed of even greater control. Partly in reaction to this a new 'independent' university has been proposed with the aid of voluntary contributions.[16] So the claim for additional resources creates a risk of loss of autonomy too. Thus a sub-system with a given measure of power will normally find that functional autonomy and the potential for development are inversely correlated; to gain more of one is to lose or risk losing some of the other. To improve its position on both parameters at once requires an improvement in the power base from which the sub-system operates.

An example of the inverse correlation between the two dimensions of freedom can be provided by an examination of the relations between professional executives and their committees in the social services.[17] Professional executives in general wish to increase their functional autonomy and therefore their control over policy decisions. This aim can be met if the committee is relatively ignorant of and indifferent to the issues involved. But such a committee is unlikely to be very interested in arguing the case with others for an increase in resources allocated to the service. Alternatively the same objective of functional autonomy may be gained by a committee whose members are strongly identified with the outlook of the professionals and prepared to trust them. While such a committee may strongly support an expansion of resources, it will be unlikely to be effective in gaining them unless it has lines of communication and influence with other groups whose frame of reference is likely to be different from that of the executive. So too narrow an identification with the executive may again limit outside influence.

So long as the executive is content with the nature and scale of the existing operations of his organisation, a passive committee will meet his needs. But many policy issues in the social services require an expansion of resources. A committee that is active and effective in securing additional resources is also likely to be more active in influencing the decisions that determine the resources required.

The committees of voluntary organisations are particularly likely to be susceptible to executive pressure to limit their control over the organisation. They are often self-selecting oligarchies, which therefore have a limited rational basis for their authority. At the same time since individual committee members participate for their own satisfaction, they are likely to resign if they face too much conflict with the executive. On the other hand voluntary organisations typically have difficulty in expanding their resources, so a condition of functional autonomy is likely to be a limited ability to expand the agency programme. These issues are clearly illustrated in Donnison's account of changes in a Canadian children's society and the London Family Welfare Association.[18]

Within the nineteenth-century economic system the large measure of functional autonomy enjoyed by the sub-systems of society did not prevent large-scale development. This may be attributed to the way in which the system helped to concentrate economic power in the hands of a minority. For those who possessed or gained this economic power, functional autonomy was exercised within very broad limits. For those who lacked it, the limits were often very narrow indeed. This narrowness was increased for some by the reluctance of society to regulate the relationships within autonomous sub-systems, whether these were economic organisations or families. In so far as intervention did occur it was to support the power of those who were already most powerful in the sub-systems, the employer in economic organisations and the father in families.

State action and the distribution of power

The change in our social system from *laissez-faire* capitalism to welfare capitalism has involved shifts in the power structure of society. Some of these power shifts have been recognised as integral to the policies being pursued. For example control of the economy to maintain a high level of employment, control of pollution, or compulsory contributions to a training levy for industry all clearly involve the exercise of power by the central government, that sets limits to the autonomy of economic and other organisations. But much of the increased power of government has arisen from its control of resources in the development of welfare provisions in which the primary objective has been seen as a redistribution of material resources. The effects on the power structure have been of secondary concern, and often scarcely acknowledged.

In so far as the shift in power created by the development of social services has been examined, the greatest attention has been given to the potential increase in the power of central government.[19] But the steadily increasing role of government in the distribution of resources has occurred in the context of a climate of opinion in which society has continued to value functional autonomy even if its priority has been somewhat reduced. The government has therefore used a wide range of expedients for redistributing resources without exercising direct control, thus changing the power structure without necessarily increasing centralisation. In pursuit of this policy the government sometimes uses existing institutions and sometimes creates semi-autonomous bodies to act as its agents. Only rarely does it provide a service itself directly to individuals. In each case varying contractual relations will affect the distribution of power.

Use of existing institutions

It has already been pointed out that if the state uses existing institutions as agents for the redistribution of resources, this tends to reinforce the original broad structural patterns of distribution, unless particular care is taken to avoid this. Similarly the use of existing institutions tends to reinforce the pre-existing internal power structure unless the conditions of the contract are designed to avoid this.

The provision of social services through employment tends to strengthen the power of the employer. For example the provision of superannuation schemes by individual employers can be a powerful means of encouraging employees to remain with them. Certainly employers have not seemed particularly interested in making schemes transferable on change of employment.[20] An older employee who cannot risk his job for fear of losing his superannuation as well will have difficulty in adopting any but the most compliant attitudes to his employer. The state has for a long time supported such schemes by providing tax allowances on the contributions. By increasing the value of the schemes it has increased the power of the employers who control them. While the government has attached conditions to the recognition of schemes, until recently the conditions were only concerned with ensuring that they were genuine superannuation schemes and the cost to the treasury was not excessive. Only when the question arose of making private schemes an alternative to the compulsory state scheme through contracting-out arrangements, was there any insistence on transferability, and retention of rights on leaving the particular employment.[21] The existence of redundancy rights related to the length of employment has a curiously ambiguous effect.[22] They sometimes lead to a sort of cat and mouse game, in which an employer who knows he will soon be faced with the need to dismiss workers may strive to make employees leave 'of their own accord', while the worker tries to hang on in increasingly uncomfortable circumstances until he is declared redundant. The provision of housing through employers, though not very common in this country except in agriculture, also strengthens the power of the employer *vis-à-vis* the employee.

The consequence of using employment as an institution for the provision of benefits can be usefully contrasted with the effect of the payment of supplementary benefits to the wives and children of employees on strike. This clearly strengthens the hand of trade unions against employers since their limited financial resources for supporting strikers are thereby increased. Equally these benefits strengthen the hands of union members against their leaders since strikers are less dependent on the union benefits if the strike is unofficial. These provisions, justified on humanitarian grounds, are opposed by those who consider that there is now too much power on the shop floor.

Similarly financial provision through the family generally tends to strengthen the position of the male 'head of the household', or at least does nothing to reduce that power. Today this particularly affects the wife since most other adults in the home receive social security benefits in their own right, thus supporting their independence of the family. It is only when the husband and wife have actually separated that the wife is entitled to supplementary benefits in her own right for herself and the children for whose maintenance she is responsible. A similar issue arises over control of the 'matrimonial home'. Until 1967 the ownership or tenancy of the home was legally regarded as belonging to one or other of the marriage partners, usually the husband, unless a joint arrangement was specifically entered into. This control of the home was often crucial in determining the power relationships within the family when major disputes arose. For example, if a wife decided that her position in the home was intolerable and the tenancy was in her husband's name, she could only separate from her husband if she had access to some other home for herself and the children, or was prepared to abandon the children. This applied to local authority tenancies as well as private tenancies. This position was changed under the Matrimonial Homes Act 1967 which gave protection to the spouse not possessing legal entitlement to the matrimonial home. If in occupation, she could only be evicted by order of a court, if not in occupation, she could gain it through a court order. Factors to be taken into consideration by the courts are the conduct of the parties and the needs of the children of the marriage.[23] Again the decision in 1945 to make family allowances payable to the mother rather than the father, which was not achieved without opposition, was clearly an attempt to influence the control of resources within the family.

One of the most controversial examples of the use of existing institutions by the state is the subsidising of voluntary bodies, and more particularly philanthropic organisations. The subsidising of mutual-benefit associations can be easily justified by a philosophy of consumer control as it is in France in the financing of the social security and health services[24] or as it was in Britain before 1948 with the Friendly Societies. But subsidising philanthropic bodies means supporting the power of small oligarchies which may be in no way representative of the tax-payer or the consumer.

Apart from paying an approximation to an economic fee for services rendered, two main methods are used for supporting philanthropic organisations. The first is a tax allowance on voluntary subscriptions to approved charities. In Britain this is confined to subscriptions covenanted for a minimum period of seven years, although in other countries the scheme may be broader in its coverage. Certain restrictions are placed on the activities of the organisation; in particular, registered charities in Britain must refrain from 'political' activity, a restriction that has come in for criticism with the changed climate of opinion in the last few years.[25] Beyond these general restrictions no controls are exercised over the use of the tax rebates. The second method is to make grants for the support of the organisation or some aspect of its work. These may be associated with some form of control, such as submission of accounts or representation on the management committee, but on the whole the controls are moral or psychological rather than direct.

Some of the arguments for using voluntary organisations to provide social services are economic. It may be cheaper to use an existing organisation than to create a new one. If the subsidy represents a small proportion of total real costs, the gain to the taxpayer may be considerable.[26] In many situations where control is not required by other considerations, an independent unit may be able to function more efficiently because it can be more flexible. Other arguments are concerned with the value of voluntary activity as such. Voluntary contributions are seen as more desirable than compulsory taxation, voluntary work as morally superior to paid employment. The wider involvement of the community implied by voluntary activity may be a useful underpinning of public support for state services.[27]

However the most influential arguments for subsidising voluntary organisations often lie paradoxically in the very fact that resources are provided without the need for political control.[28] Sometimes it is the need to demonstrate the independence of the organisation from state control because the people whom it serves are rightly or wrongly suspicious of the attitude of the authorities to them. Examples are the work of the Family Service Units with problem families[29] and the Simon

Community with adult drop-outs.[30] Sometimes it is because a majority of the electorate, or a vocal minority might attempt to impose controls which would negate the objectives of the service. There is a long tradition that 'pioneering' new services is more appropriate for voluntary bodies than for governmental organisations. Such a tradition must rest on a belief that political control is inimical to some forms of innovation. Finally many professions have resisted political control and their services have only been made available to the state on condition that normal political controls are avoided. An example of this is the administration of the legal aid scheme by the Law Society.

Semi-autonomous state organisations

As an intermediate stage between the use of existing institutions and the direct provision of services, the state may create semi-autonomous bodies which it either finances wholly or to which it gives power to raise its own resources through taxation or charges. The arguments used to justify the creation of such bodies tend to be precisely similar to those used for subsidising voluntary bodies, except that there is either no suitable voluntary body in existence, or the political importance of the issues makes complete independence impossible. The Race Relations Board and the Community Relations Commission have to demonstrate freedom from external political pressures to retain the confidence of the blacks, while the government must ensure that the quality of their personnel is such that the public at large will also accept it.[31] The old regional hospital boards and the new area health boards were created largely because of the fears of the medical profession of close political control.[32] The Young Volunteer Force Foundation was created to encourage voluntary activity among young people.[33]

With bodies such as these which are created by government and wholly financed by it, political control is much more readily asserted under pressure. For example the regional hospital boards were never given the freedom that was originally intended because of the need to control their rapidly increasing expenditure.[34] The Probation and After-Care Service is ostensibly run by committees composed of magistrates. At one time the probation committees really were autonomous. As the government has felt increasingly obliged to ensure that the services attained adequate standards, more and more control has passed to the Home Office.[35]

Of these semi-autonomous agents of government, the local authorities are far the most important in Britain today, because of the large resources they administer, the range of their activities, and the politically sensitive nature of some of these, such as housing, education and planning. Local authorities are clearly agents of government. They are created by Act of Parliament and can only undertake activities sanctioned by Act of Parliament. Equally they can be compelled to make certain provisions and if they fail to do so, the relevant services can be undertaken by central government and the cost charged to the local authority. On the other hand the authorities have considerable independence in the way they carry out their duties and the extent to which they undertake permissive activities. This independence in matters of such importance is justified by the fact that they raise some of their own funds by local taxation and are accountable for administering their resources to a popular electorate.[36]

Over many years fears have been expressed that the independence of local authorities from central government control has been steadily eroded.[37] Much of this discussion has taken place in the absence of hard facts about the degree of control that is exercised by central government in practice. This gap has been partially filled recently by certain studies of which that by Griffith[38] is perhaps the most important. Griffith examined the working of the system in relation to six specific services: primary and secondary school-building, highways, housing, planning, children's services and health and welfare services. He found that the extent of external control exercised was influenced more by the political importance of the services than by their relative efficiency or inefficiency. But equally important was the philosophy of the government departments concerned. Griffith found evidence of three different approaches: a laissez-faire approach typified by the attitude of the Ministry of Health to health and welfare services; a regulatory approach shown in the Home Office attitude to children's services; and a promotional approach exemplified by the attitude of HM Inspectors of Education.[39] The first and third of these approaches, in so far as control is exercised at all, imply the use of authority rather than power. Even the Home Office approach is largely based on the enforcement of minimum standards, and it has been argued earlier such minimum standards are justified on a policy of minimum interference with the independence of the authorities.[40]

One of the reasons given for anxiety about the independence of local authorities has been their increasing reliance on central government finance. Boaden[41] has tested five hypotheses that would follow if the autonomy of local authorities was limited by central government pressure founded on financial dependence. His first hypothesis for example is that local authorities within any particular class of authority will display broadly similar levels of activity within any service area, and his fourth that within any class of local authority, poorer authorities in terms of financial resources will be more likely to conform to central wishes and submit to central control. Boaden found the evidence was against all five hypotheses.

There is some evidence of increased control in certain services. The Labour government of 1964–70 attempted to enforce the speedy development of comprehensive secondary education, but this policy was reversed by the succeeding Conservative government.[42] The Conservatives passed legislation controlling the rent policies of local authorities, which is strongly opposed by Labour.[43] But many examples can be found in the opposite direction. The first breach in the *ultra vires* rule which forbids local authorities to spend money on any activities which are not specifically authorised by Act of Parliament was made in 1963 when local authorities were allowed to spend up to the value of a penny rate on any object that was for the benefit of the area or its inhabitants.[44]

The fact is that both expediency and ideology in Britain are against a high level of central control over local authorities. This situation can be contrasted with that in France where the national civil service interpenetrates local administration to a considerable degree. The prefect, for instance, who is the administrative head of the local services in his area, is an officer of the national civil service and directly accountable to central government. This system, devised by Napoleon, was based on a much older tradition of centralisation.[45]

Direct provision

In this climate of opinion in Britain it becomes necessary to justify direct provision by central government rather than the other way round. The sort of arguments that are used can best be illustrated by an example such as the administration of social security. At the time that Beveridge prepared the report on which the system of social security was based in 1948, benefits were paid through a variety of different organisations and systems. This created inconvenience to individuals, duplication of payments and gaps in provision, and in some cases lack of certainty in obtaining benefits.[46] These disadvantages could have been largely removed if the system had been unified but transferred to local authorities. Other considerations determined that it should be a national organisation; first, the need for uniformity of benefit rates and conditions; second, for uniformity of procedures; third, for avoidance of demarcation problems and fourth, for economies of scale.[47] These are primarily issues concerned with the distribution of resources. Finally there was the problem of the distribution of costs and the control over expenditure. Since territorial justice required that costs should be met nationally, control over expenditure also demanded national control.[48]

These are the arguments that are recorded in the Beveridge Report. A final issue, not mentioned in the report, was that the political importance of social security, in view of experience in the inter-war years, was such that the central government could not trust local authorities with responsibility for this service.

In general national administration by central government is likely to be dictated by the political sensitivity of the service, the need for uniformity of provision, the need for control over costs, and the value of economies of scale.

Contractual conditions

Earlier it was pointed out that the degree of functional autonomy exercised by a sub-system depended on the nature of the contract under which it received its resources. Chester,[49] examining grants from central government to local authorities, suggested that these could be classified by their position on five separate criteria:

1 Conditional—unconditional: Is payment of the grant made dependent on the fulfilment of certain conditions, or is it unconditional?

2 Specific—general: Is the grant given in respect of a particular operation or activity of a local authority or for the whole or a major part of its activities?

3 Variable—fixed: Does or does not the amount of the grant to the individual local authority vary promptly with the level of activity of that authority? The variable grant can either be based on a unit of service such as the number of people assisted or the number of homes built or be paid as a percentage of total expenditure on a service. In either case a maximum may be set.

4 Means-related—uniform: Does the level of the grant vary with the means of the local authority or is it uniform to all local authorities irrespective of their means?

5 In kind—in cash: This is really a variant of the specific-general criterion, with payment in kind representing the most specific type of grant.

This classification can be applied to other forms of grant or payment, but to apply it more generally two other variables have to be included, which do not apply to the type of grant Chester was considering.

6 Discretionary—of right: Is the grant discretionary or must it be paid if certain objective criteria are fulfilled?

7 Transfer payment—economic payment: Is it a payment for services rendered comparable to a payment in the context of the economic market or is it a transfer payment?

Most grants can be classified effectively by these criteria. Thus family allowances are unconditional, in that they can be used in any way the family desires; specific; variable in relation to the number of children although not to the activity in respect of them; uniform between different families regardless of means; in cash; of right; and a transfer payment. Free school meals on the other hand are conditional on attendance at school; specific; variable in relation to the number of children attending school; means dependent; in kind; generally of right; and a transfer payment.

It is clear that in terms of the effect of the grant on functional autonomy, the most crucial question is the first, whether conditions are attached to the use or receipt of the grant, and if so the extent. Other criteria are more limited in their effect. Specific grants and grants in kind only limit autonomy in the specific area to which the grants apply. They can be either accepted or rejected, but neither course need lead to additional controls unless other conditions are attached to the grant. Similarly variable grants can be used to encourage activity in some or even in all directions, but they still leave the most important choices to the grant receiver. Means grants may have an opposite effect in discouraging activities that might raise income. This is not true of means-related grants to local authorities since means are assessed on the basis of rateable value which represents potential not actual income. No limit is normally placed by the central government on the amount of money raised by local authorities through the rates.

Where payments are made for services rendered, like payments to voluntary bodies for the care of children or residential facilities for old people, control if exercised at all is limited to control over the quality of the service provided.

If conditions are attached to a grant they can be very pervasive going far beyond the particular area to which at first sight the grant seems relevant. So social services departments have a discretionary power to give financial assistance to families with a view to preventing the children from having to be taken into care. A family requesting assistance with rent arrears to prevent eviction, might quite legitimately be required to review their whole budgeting procedures to ensure that the same difficulty did not arise again. Similarly the Labour government in the late 1960s used control over the school-building programme as a means of forcing local authorities to move more quickly towards a comprehensive system of secondary education. Such conditions are particularly powerful weapons of control if the need is great and the grant is a recurring one. Discretionary grants give power to those who dispense them not by their nature, but because conditions may be explicitly or implicitly attached to the grant, or even only be believed to be attached to it—for example the belief that a grant will not in fact be given unless the applicant adopts the right compliant attitudes.

Chapter 7
Professionalism and the structure of the social services

Summary of the argument

This chapter examines the strategies and tactics used by professional workers with rational-pragmatic authority in attempting to expand their influence while retaining functional autonomy.

Professionalism is seen as an ideology used to legitimate the power, authority and status of certain occupational groups. In furthering their interests and ideals these groups have two alternative or complementary strategies open to them. The first is based on a professional association controlling the standards of entry to practice. It is particularly relevant to professionals working as independent practitioners within the economic market, and favours individual functional authority. The second is based on the control of organisations employing professionals and favours expansion of the opportunities for development sometimes at the expense of individual autonomy.

The conflict between professional and bureaucratic norms, to which much attention is given in sociological studies, is seen as basically an issue of socialisation, which is common to others who are employed in organisations. Similarly the search for functional autonomy is also an example of a broader social phenomenon.

In attempting to maintain functional autonomy three main strategies are used—a policy of withdrawal or segmentation, a policy of spreading risks, and the reorganisation of the larger system. Segmentation is a particularly common strategy in the social services.

The effect of the search for professional autonomy on the structure of the social services has been organisational specialisation on the basis of skills. This has created major problems of co-ordination in planning provision and in meeting the specific needs of individuals. 'Management' is only a partial solution. A reorganisation on the basis of interprofessional teams may ultimately provide an answer, but a prerequisite of this may be changes in professional education.

Professionalism

Sociological studies of professionalism have generally followed three main approaches. First there have been attempts to define a profession and to measure the degree of professionalism of different occupations. Second there have been studies of the process of professionalisation. Third, attention has been directed to relations between professionals and administrators in bureaucratic organisations. To some extent the validity of the last two approaches depends on the validity of the first. In fact sociologists are becoming increasingly doubtful of the value of the concept of a 'profession'.

A good example of attempts to define the nature of a profession is provided by Greenwood.[1] He listed five characteristics of the ideal profession: a systematic body of theory, professional authority, the sanction of the community, a regulative code of ethics and a professional culture. Etzioni[2] has a somewhat similar list and defines as 'semi-professions' those aspiring occupations which lack one or more of the attributes he lists.

The limitation of this approach lies in the fact that none of the criteria are specific to occupations that are recognised as professions. Turner and Hodge[3] have gone so far as to say that the characteristics attributed to professions are more effective in distinguishing between different professions than between professions and non-professions.

What appears to have happened in this case, as in some others, is that sociologists have taken a lay term and attempted to give it precision. This has led to difficulties because lay usage is very vague indeed, and its most important common denominator is probably its status element. Professions are given that title by the general public because they are high status occupations rather than because they fulfil the criteria listed by Greenwood or Etzioni.

Carr-Saunders and Wilson[4] have commented that in the eighteenth century the dominant characteristic of those occupations recognised as professions was that they were regarded as suitable occupations for the younger sons of the gentry. In their view this was a temporary aberration, and both before and after this period greater recognition was given to the nature and importance of the skills exercised. However the importance of theory as against skills is a comparatively recent phenomenon. Jamous and Peloille[5] have argued that even today the basis of professional authority is not the system of theory but the element of 'mystery' that makes the knowledge esoteric.

This problem becomes particularly clear when one examines studies of the process of professionalisation. Caplow,[6] for example, lists four stages in the process beginning with the establishment of a professional association with definite membership criteria designed to keep out the unqualified, and ending with a prolonged political agitation whose object is to obtain the support of the public power for the maintenance of the new occupational barriers. While this may be the commonest approach today, it is completely alien to some of the oldest professions that have established and maintained their position, not through a professional association but through control of the organisation that employs them. This is true for example of the churches, of the armed forces and of universities.[7] Thus there are two bases for occupational power neither of which is exclusive to professionals.

These arguments suggest that a profession can most usefully be regarded as an occupational group that possesses or aspires to high status based on rational-pragmatic authority. Professionalism should then be regarded not so much as an ideal but as an ideology whose function is to legitimate the power, authority and status of such occupational groups. These are the senses in which the words will be used in the rest of this chapter.

The fact that professionalism is regarded in this light is not to deny validity to the claims of professionals to authority or to deny the importance of professional ideals in influencing the behaviour of professionals. Doctors, teachers and social workers do have knowledge and skills which are useful to society. They do promote ideals such as improved health, cultural and educational values, and social concern for the disadvantaged. Enhancing their power and authority helps to spread the use of these skills and to ensure that the values receive more adequate expression in society. But it also promotes their own personal interests, and it is often very difficult for outsiders as well as the professionals themselves to distinguish clearly when self-interest is taking preference over ideals in their advocacy of a particular course.

The professional association as a power base

The power of professional associations rests primarily on their ability to assert a monopoly control over particular skills and knowledge. In performing this function their role is very similar to that of trade unions. Many professional associations are in fact scarcely distinguishable from trade unions in the methods they employ, or indeed are able to employ in exerting pressure on outsiders to protect their interests. Such associations have been termed by Harries-Jenkins 'protective associations',[8] and there are two main types. In the first of these the membership is open to all those performing certain functions regardless of their qualifications. They are sometimes called 'occupational associations'. Examples are the National Association of Probation Officers and the Association of University Teachers. The second type of protective association is only open to those with certain qualifications as the British Medical Association is only open to qualified doctors, and the British Association of Social Workers to social workers with specific qualifications.

The formation of a protective association of qualified members is seen by Caplow[9] as the first stage of professionalisation. But the power of such an association is likely to be limited unless it can gain control over entry into practice, and this is particularly necessary if practice is conducted in a competitive economic situation. This is well illustrated by the position of general medical practitioners in the nineteenth century.[10] Although under the Medical Act 1858 the body subsequently known as the General Medical Council was appointed to keep a register of all qualified medical practitioners, general practitioners themselves had no means of controlling the numbers entering general practice. Medical schools were controlled by

Fellows of the Royal College of Physicians and Members of the Royal College of Surgeons who had a direct financial interest in increasing the numbers of students that they taught. Neither did the legislation restrict medical practice to those who were on the register. So there was considerable competition from others with lesser or no qualifications who had no inhibitions about offering a cheaper service of poorer quality. It was to meet this situation that the British Medical Association was founded but it had little success in this direction for many years. Its greatest triumph in the nineteenth century was to improve the conditions of service of doctors employed by local and poor law authorities, by a policy of blacklisting those who offered employment on poor conditions. As a result the standard of living of most general practitioners in this period was extremely low, and they were often forced to provide a poor quality of medical care and even to engage in unethical practices. It was only when the state became actively interested in the promotion of a health programme during the negotiations that led up to the National Health Insurance Act 1911 that the BMA came into its own. It successfully negotiated a scheme which enabled general practitioners to receive income from the state without renouncing the advantages of independence. It was the exclusion from these sources of income of those who were unregistered that first effectively protected qualified doctors from 'unfair competition'.

While the ideal model for professional practice is often seen as independent operation within the terms of the economic market, in which functional autonomy is high, it is not difficult to see why professionals often find the rigours of full competition unacceptable. The risks of loss of income, the pressures to exploit the ignorance of clients, and the dangers that in consequence public confidence may be undermined, all provide good reasons for asserting professional control over standards of entry and of practice, and if possible over numbers. The state also has an interest in protecting standards of entry and practice, but is likely to have difficulty in doing so where the service is dominated by numerous independent practitioners, unless it has the co-operation of the professionals themselves. Thus the stage is set for a contract between the state and the profession, which generally leads to what has become known as a qualifying association, an association which is given power by the state to control entry into the profession and to some extent engagement in practice.

However, despite the convergence of interest between society represented by the state and the profession, their interests never fully coincide. The profession is likely to want to raise the standards of entry so as to restrict numbers and maintain their exclusiveness and the privileges that go with it, when the public interest may require a larger entry even at the expense of lower standards. Similarly while state and profession will both have an interest in the maintenance of standards of conduct and practice after qualification, the interest of the profession is likely to be tempered both by concern for the freedom of individual practitioners and by the loyalty of colleagueship.

The organisation as a professional power base

The alternative to the qualifying association as a professional power base is control over the organisations that employ members of the profession. Attention has already been drawn to the use of this by the hierarchies of the armed forces, the established churches and the universities. To a lesser extent the power of the Royal Colleges in the medical field in the nineteenth century rested on their control of access to the hospitals, and this is even more true today of the power of consultants and specialists. Even the power of barristers has depended on their ability to control access to the courts whose government has been kept in the hands of their own members.

Control of organisations like these is an extremely powerful tool in the hands of professionals for promoting their interests and ideals. An organisation can exercise control over those whom it employs through its ability to give and withhold resources, and to provide opportunities for practising skills and achieving status and income through promotion. Such controls can be used, and often are, to limit the freedom of professionals. But equally, in the hands of fellow professionals, they can be used to support professional ideals and standards in all aspects of practice, and to limit the destructive competition that is endemic in private practice. An organisation is also better placed than independent practitioners to claim control over capital resources from society. This in turn increases its control over those who want access to the resources, and aids the establishment of at least a partial monopoly.

Organisational power is particularly favourable to progress along what I have earlier called the second dimension of freedom (pp. 105–6), namely the expansion of potential achievements. The organisation makes possible an increased access to resources; increased specialisation within a co-ordinated system; the development of new skills; and a career structure that aids personal development. Moreover by the allocation of tasks according to ability and the exercise of control over the less skilled, it becomes possible to employ people with a wide range of skills with minimum danger to standards in both the short and the long run. This removes one of the major conflicts of interest that occur between society and professional associations in that professionals have less incentive to restrict entry into practice to an extent that cuts across the needs of society as a whole.

Professional control of an organisation is of course, much more favourable to group than to individual functional autonomy. Many differences can arise between the lower and the higher echelons of the organisation, some at least of which will be related to professional standards. To protect the interests of the lower echelons a protective association, and particularly an occupational association may be more appropriate than a qualifying association.

Professionals in formal organisations

Sociologists have paid considerable attention to conflicts between professional norms and the hierarchical and bureaucratic structure of formal organisations. In view of the importance of organisational power in the development of many professions, the basis of this conflict is of some interest.

First, it is important to note that bureaucratic and professional norms have much in common. Blau and Scott[11] for example list six characteristics of professionalism and all but one of these are also characteristic of the ideal bureaucrat.

Both base their decisions on the application of universalistic principles to particular cases; for both specialisation is the key to expertise and status is dependent on achievement and not ascription; for both the relationships with clients are marked by affective neutrality; for both self-interest must be subjugated to other principles. The divergence lies in the sixth characteristic, the ultimate source of authority.

The ultimate source of authority for the professional lies outside the formal organisation that employs him in the body of his professional colleagues or in the training institution in which he learnt his standards. For the bureaucrat ultimate authority lies in the hierarchical structure of the organisation. This problem is perhaps more accurately identified by Abrahamson[12] who sees the main issue in the process of socialisation which can prepare people more or less adequately for working within an organisation. This is, of course, a universal truth that applies to other employees besides professionals, so that ultimately problems in the management of professionals are similar to those in the management of other workers.

The two extreme methods of minimising conflict between organisation and professionals are to socialise professionals within the organisation or to structure the organisation to meet the needs of the professional. The first is relatively common, although as professions develop, there is an increasing tendency to split off educational functions into separate departments or institutions. This gives greater opportunity for divergence. The opposite extreme is less common, and the universities represent one of the few examples of this approach on a large scale.[13] An organisation that maximises functional autonomy for the individual in the way that the university tries to do is extremely difficult to control. Co-ordination, as opposed to sporadic co-operation, becomes almost impossible. Change also becomes extremely difficult, because it becomes dependent on achieving agreement between a large number of individuals whose views and interests will frequently conflict. As a result most developments are likely to be based on the maintenance of the *status quo* as far as possible.

In most professions there is a compromise. Academic teaching is combined with some form of apprenticeship. Hopefully this produces a creative conflict, in which new entrants to the profession are enabled to work in an organisation, but at the same time take sufficient new ideas from the independent training institution to the organisation to make it flexible in its response to change. However, this is not likely to work out unless there is mutual respect, understanding and influence between the teaching institution and the organisations which employ the professionals. Without this, there is danger that a professional will either reject his training or reject the organisation.

The most extreme case of divergence of norms between professional and organisation occurs when the organisation attempts to use the skill of a professional for purposes that are contrary to professional ethics or in ways that will destroy the basis of public confidence in the profession. Teachers, research workers and journalists, individually and collectively resist pressure to suppress or distort the truth; doctors resist attempts to use their skills to manipulate their clients against the interests of the latter. Much more common are those marginal cases where the issues revolve round the relative weight to be given to different factors in the situation. Such conflicts, of course, occur as frequently between members of different professions, or even of the same profession, as between professionals and administrators.

Three major concerns of management that particularly affect the freedom of professionals are the need to control the allocation of scarce resources; the need for co-ordination of interdependent activities; and the need for supervision of the quality of performance, including the speed of work.

Scarcity of resources inevitably sets limits on the work of professionals. If control over resources is delegated to the individual worker he knows the limits within which he must work and has freedom to decide for himself the best methods of allocation. But if too many resources are allocated to a lower level, there is little possibility of flexible readjustment to meet special needs or new situations. The scarcer resources are in relation to demand the more necessary it will be to retain control at a higher level. An example of this is provided by the control exercised in children's departments over foster-parent placements and places in children's homes. If individual officers are given control over certain placements, they are in a good position to assess the relative importance of the needs of different clients, but it is much more difficult for them to take into account the needs of others. A senior officer is likely to have less complete information about cases but more objectivity in making decisions.[14] Another example of this is the control of beds by consultants. To meet the consultants' demand for functional autonomy, they are generally allocated control of a number of beds. This creates problems in meeting short-term emergencies and in enabling the system to adjust to long-term changes in the need for hospitalisation for particular types of illness or treatment.[15]

One of the most important needs of management is to keep expenditure within the limits of the budget. It is relatively easy to delegate to the worker control over the use of his own time for which total cost is fixed by salary (unless payment is made for overtime). Responsibility for control of resources can also be delegated if some limit can be placed on the cost. It is particularly difficult to delegate responsibility where demand and cost are potentially unlimited. This is why the panel system adopted by general practitioners allows more functional autonomy than would be possible under a system of payment by item of service. Under the panel system general practitioners have complete freedom in the use of their time, at least as long as no complaints are made by patients about the quality of service they receive. On the other hand, because the costs of prescriptions are potentially unlimited, some controls are regarded as necessary.[16]

The need to co-ordinate interdependent activities is another function of management that may create conflict. Specialisation increases the opportunities for productive action and in this sense contributes to an increase in freedom, but it also increases the dependence on others. Poor co-ordination will restrict the advantages of specialisation and even make it counterproductive. Such co-ordination can be achieved through voluntary co-operation, but there may be considerable difficulty in reconciling conflicting value systems from a position of equality. Hence the importance of hierarchy and at the same time the basis for its rejection.[17]

To some extent the conflicts with management raised by co-ordination and the allocation of scarce resources are based on differences of perspective rather than fundamental issues. The interest of the professional is concentrated on more limited objectives than management because of his concern with particular clients and particular processes. The supervision of the quality of performance raises deeper personal issues which may affect both the professional's self-esteem and his material prospects. This makes the conflicts much more difficult to resolve. A compromise is sometimes used. It may be tolerable or even welcome to have a dependent relationship on a superior if it helps to reduce anxiety where decisions are particularly difficult or crucial, or if it is seen as contributing to the development of skills. So quality control may be combined with these more positive objectives to make it more acceptable. An example of this is provided by the use of supervision in social work.[18] However the compromise may not be successful if anxiety about control outweighs the advantages of support.

Strategies for increasing functional autonomy

At the centre of the issue of socialisation lies the pressure for functional autonomy that is built up by the training which many professionals receive. A long period of education, often within an institution geared to the questioning of established truths, is combined with a training that sets high ideals of practice which may bear little relation to actual conditions of work. How then do professionals attempt to establish functional autonomy within the organisations in which they must work?

Gouldner,[19] examining the problem in general terms, identified three strategies which can be used by a part of a larger system or organisation to increase its autonomy. The first is a strategy of withdrawal which can be achieved if the part ensures that it maintains the capacity to service its minimal needs. This strategy is closely allied to the process of segmentation discussed by Hammond and Mitchell,[20] though they approach it as a method by which the organisation manages conflict rather than the other way round. Segmentation involves creating a separate structure within which the professional group can work independently, usually with a fellow professional as administrative head.

The second strategy identified by Gouldner is one of spreading risks so that need can be met from several alternative sources. An extension of this strategy is to try to ensure that authority over the part is divided between two or more groups whose interests are not identical. This makes possible the familiar procedure of playing one authority against the other according to need.

Gouldner's third strategy is the most radical. It is to undertake a reorganisation of the larger system to ensure that the distinctive needs of the part receive a higher priority.

Segmentation and withdrawal

A successful policy for maintaining functional autonomy by withdrawal or segmentation can be achieved through the pursuit of a number of secondary goals.

1   Financial and capital resources should be obtained with as few recurrent controls as possible, and the continued right to them should if possible be inalienable. This implies a preference for controls that approximate more closely to the generalised norms of society, particularly those of the economic market as against full integration into the structure of the public authority. Voluntary committees and appointed boards represent intermediate situations. The progressive advantages of these different systems of control are partly due to the relative autonomy associated with resources owned or earned, or received as gifts, as compared with those obtained through compulsory taxation. A related but separate issue is the nature of the authority and the frame of reference of the interstitial committee. The authority of a voluntary committee is limited in the ways discussed in the previous chapter. Both the appointed board and the voluntary committee, particularly if they include professional representation, are likely to have closer relationships with the executive than with the wider public of contributors and consumers. Thus the committee will tend to become identified with the objectives of the executive and be more easily manipulated by them than a committee accountable to a democratic electorate, which will be more sensitive to political issues.

2   Necessary supportive services should be within the control

of the sub-system. To this end it will try to gain exclusive control over accommodation and other capital resources. It will employ its own specialists instead of making use of the specialist services provided by other sub-systems—avoiding for example typing pools and common administrative services.

This often involves the employment of professional workers in organisations and departments controlled by other professions, creating a problem of functional autonomy for the dominated group. Social workers have particularly suffered from this, under medical control and in educational services. Medical social workers in hospitals have constantly complained about the limited role assigned to them in hospitals.[21] Local authority social workers in departments controlled by medical officers of health often had similar experiences.[22] The educational welfare service has never been allowed to develop into a social-work service, that could serve the broad social interests of children and their families.[23] A similar problem arises in educational institutions, where lecturers are employed in departments to teach supporting subjects. Such lecturers find limited opportunities for promotion and for the development of their own subjects.

Where specialist and technical resources cannot be included in the sub-system, some control can be retained if the transaction is of mutual advantage as when a cash payment is made for the service.

3 Programmes that involve co-operation with other sub-systems should be avoided. If they cannot be avoided, the respective responsibilities should be clearly defined.

4 Interest should be withdrawn from the rewards that might follow involvement in the larger systems. It sometimes seems surprising to what extent professional workers are able to content themselves with the limited objectives imposed on them by their demand for functional autonomy. Lortie[24] shows how primary school teachers in America retain their sense of independence because they do not want promotion or to influence policy. The functional autonomy of probation officers is dependent on restricting their functions to social casework and having no control over custodial or residential care, in contrast to social workers in the children's services.[25] General practitioners, though seeking greater access to resources and

facilities have shown little enthusiasm for the potential benefits of a broader co-ordination of social and medical services.[26]
One reason for this appears to be that professionals may have
a closer emotional identification with the practice of particular skills than with the broader ends to which the skills
are means. Doctors, social workers and teachers seem more
concerned to have opportunities to practise medical, casework or teaching skills than to pursue broader goals of rehabilitation or education except in so far as their specialist skills
can contribute to this.[27]

5 For the professional worker, the values of his profession
must be dominant at all levels of the organisation. Lower levels
must be controlled by members of the profession, higher levels
infiltrated and influenced. Hence the importance of the voluntary or appointed committee, and the departmentalism of local
authorities. The latter is of particular interest because one
would expect the demand for a co-ordinated policy to over-
ride such sectional interests. Yet the pressure for a departmental structure based on occupational skills, with each
department having its own committee seems in the past to
have been irresistible.[28] Perhaps the resultant functional
autonomy meets the needs of councillors as well as professionals. In the field of social work the development of separate
departments has been part of a deliberate strategy for professional development, as is described later.

6 For the front-line professional worker the sub-system
should be kept as small as possible, compatible with professional
objectives—ideally a separate sub-system for each professional
worker. Where large organisations are required to provide and
control technical plant and accommodate multiple specialisa-
tions, this may lead to departmentalism based on specialisation. This can be clearly seen in the structure of hospitals and
universities. In hospitals each consultant and specialist leads
his 'firm', and his position is confirmed by his control of beds.[29]
In universities the Robbins Committee reported that the average size of departments is about nine staff.[30] Each department
tends to offer an honours degree in its own subject. Degrees
with a wider subject base are less common though they might
meet the needs of students better.

To limit the power of higher administrative levels over the

small departments, conventions and rules are developed in the manner described by Crozier.[31] Government by committees of equals representing the vested interests of the participants tends to ensure that resources are divided in a way that supports the *status quo*. This puts severe limits on the potential for change.

Some of the problems created for professionals by a policy of segmentation are discussed by Barber.[32] He draws attention to the difficulty that is often experienced of finding a head for the professional enclave who is both highly qualified professionally and an effective administrator. But the greatest problem is that segmentation is likely to inhibit communication with the wider system and therefore to reduce the influence on it of the professionals in the segmented structure. In the social services it can be seen to limit the claim on additional resources of those with less power, to hinder the co-ordination of inter-dependent decisions and the development of joint activities, and to lessen professional influence on the referral system and therefore control over the work performed.

Segmentation, which has been the commonest strategy used by professionals in maintaining professional freedom, thus emphasises functional autonomy at the expense of expansion and development. While this policy may be short-sighted from the point of view of professionals, it is far more serious for clients in its total effect on the quality of services they receive. Comment has already been made on this in discussing the consequences of defining need in terms of specific techniques and in the chapter on co-ordination.

Spreading risks

There are two ways in which a sub-system can increase its functional autonomy by spreading risks. The first is by having a variety of sources for finance and other necessary resources. The private practitioner has many independent paying clients and in the ordinary way has little need to placate any one of them. General practitioners in panel practice under the National Health Insurance Act 1911 avoided total dependence on the state scheme by engaging in private practice, while the panel scheme itself divided responsibility between the

Health Insurance Committees and numerous panel patients.[33] General practitioners under the National Health Service are somewhat more restricted by their loss of private practice and their loss of the right to sell their panel practice. Universities have found it harder to resist government control as other sources of finance, such as fees from private sources and voluntary contributions, have failed to keep pace with the expansion promoted by the government.[34]

The second way of spreading risks, which may be related to sources of finance, but is not necessarily so, is to have more than one source of authority. The Probation and After-Care Service has two sources of finance, central government and local authorities, but these sources are complementary rather than alternative sources—each pays an agreed 50 per cent of the cost of the service—so this does not necessarily increase functional autonomy. But the service does have alternative sources of authority to which appeal can be made, of which the most important are the Home Office and the probation committees composed of magistrates.[35] Individual officers are often in an even better position. If there is doubt about the legitimacy of any course of action a probation officer wishes to pursue, he can choose between consulting the magistrates in court or in a case committee, the justice's clerk as the legal expert, or the professional hierarchy of the service, according to which of these he thinks will give the answer he wants. There are disadvantages in serving more than one master but it can make possible a measure of freedom through playing one off against another.

Reorganisation of the larger system

Reorganisation of the larger system to ensure that the distinctive needs of the part received a higher priority has been most clearly exemplified in recent years in the development of the local authority social-work services. The emergence of social work as an effective influence in local authority services began with the creation of the children's departments in 1948. The strategy used then on the recommendation of the Curtis Committee[36] proved a useful model for future development.

Before 1948 responsibility for the care of children deprived of normal family support was distributed among several bodies with differing functions and different criteria for determining the standards of care. The largest group of children in this situation were those in the care of local authorities under the Poor Law. They were the responsibility of the public assistance committees, served by 'relieving officers' trained as clerks and administrators not social workers. Other children had been placed under fit person orders to the local education authorities. The approved schools, though under the supervision of the Home Office children's departments, were seen as primarily educational or penal institutions. Some children at risk were under the supervision of local authority health departments; others were under the national Ministry of Pensions. Almost none of these bodies employed staff with a social-work training to supervise or care for the children.

The Curtis Committee found the most disquieting evidence of neglect in the care of many of these children particularly of their social and emotional needs. Its recommendations, largely put into effect through the Children Act 1948, were designed to make social-work values dominant in their care. Under the Act most of the relevant functions were concentrated in a single local authority department with its own committee, with a children's officer whose suitability would be approved by the Home Office. At central government level the Home Office children's department provided overall policy, and, through its inspectors, supervision of the children's departments, voluntary children's homes, approved schools and the development of training.

In 1948 the shortage of appropriately qualified workers at all levels from the inspectorate to child care officers was a considerable block to the aims of the Curtis Committee.[37] Over the next twenty years with the expansion of training, particularly after 1960, this problem was diminished and qualified social workers took increasing responsibility for the standards of the service. But the shortage at field level was never solved as the responsibilities of the local departments expanded almost as fast as the recruitment and training of new workers.[38]

Over this same period of twenty years the problem took on a new perspective as social workers employed in many different situations, including the children's departments, began to chafe against the restrictions imposed by departmental structures. The limited functions of departments meant that effective social work which took into account all the interdependent needs of individuals and families was impossible. Children's departments could not undertake work to save children coming into care. Social workers had to share responsibility for the same families, and stop helping as soon as particular tasks were completed. Trained social workers in local authority health departments found that medical control meant that social-work criteria for action were discounted. In welfare departments the administrative values of the Poor Law often still determined procedures. Child care officers were frequently in conflict with the decisions of courts and subject to their overriding jurisdiction.

The original lever for change was provided by a much more general public concern about the treatment of juvenile delinquents. The public was worried by the incidence of juvenile crime yet often combined this with an almost sentimental reluctance to take action against the children concerned. Social work offered an attractive compromise, preventive action that was oriented to the welfare of the child. This course was supported by psychologists, criminologists and others who felt that the courts could not avoid a damaging penal approach to delinquent children.

The delinquency lobby and the social-work lobby managed to get under way a series of committees to examine the issues that concerned them, At first the primary focus was given to delinquency in the Ingleby, Kilbrandon and Longford Reports.[39] Later the reorganisation of social work as such gained equal importance with the establishment of the Seebohm Committee.[40] Finally the issues were resolved by two legislative acts. First, the Children and Young Persons Act 1969 transferred major decision-making responsibilities for delinquents from the courts to social workers. Soon after, the Local Authority Social Services Act 1971 concentrated the social-work functions of local authorities in a single department. The same strategy was used as in the Children Act twenty years before. Local authorities, were compelled by the Act to set up separate 'social services' departments under their own committees. The appointment of the chief executive of the departments was again subject to the approval of the central government—in this case the Department of Health and Social Security. Essentially this was a strategy of segmentation on a larger scale.

The structure of social services

The search for professional autonomy has encouraged the segmentation of social services on the basis of specialist skills and knowledge. The principle received formal government approval in Britain when proposals were put forward around 1970 for the reorganisation of health and social-work services. On the questions raised by the division of responsibility between the proposed area health boards and the local authorities, the Green Paper, *The Future Structure of the National Health Service* stated: 'After carefully considering the contrasting views expressed on these questions, the Government has decided that the services should be organised according to the main skills required to provide them rather than by any categorisation of primary user.'[41]

This was the principle that was followed in subsequent legislation. It is a principle that has in the past helped to create major problems of co-ordination.[42]

The same conflicts that have resulted in the segmentation of the social services, have also made it difficult for those with different skills to co-operate in working for individual clients. Workers throughout the services, and not least those with professional education, fail to recognise the limits of their own knowledge in meeting the needs of their clients; fail to appreciate the importance of the values held by others; and fail to respect the knowledge and skills of those with different backgrounds.

One solution to this has been sought in the concept of 'management'. This has been an important theme in many reports though as often concerned with the work of specific services as with interservice co-ordination.[43] There is no doubt that management techniques will have an important contribution to make to the efficiency of the social services, but there is always the danger that by increasing the importance of the upper echelons of the hierarchy, the responsibility, initiative and flexibility of the front-line workers may be impaired.

The Maud Committee on management in local government attempted in its proposals to reconcile these contradictory interests.[44] To further interdepartmental co-ordination it proposed that a small management board should be appointed by each local authority council from its own members, which would be responsible to the council for the development of policy. The management board's chief executive would be a clerk, not necessarily, as now, with legal qualifications, to whom the principal officers of departments would be responsible. This would tend to concentrate power in the hands of a small group of councillors and the clerk, reducing the power of departmental heads and of the majority of elected members. To redress the balance new committees, which would no longer have executive powers, would examine policy, call for reports, and make recommendation to the management board. The principal officers in charge of departments would have direct access to their committees, which would in turn be part of the main council as well as having representation on the management board, and would limit the power of the clerk over the principal officers. At the same time the committee recommended that local authorities 'should adopt the guiding principle that issues are dealt with at the lowest level consistent with the nature of the problem'.[45]

Such a policy would undoubtedly improve the co-ordination of provision. There is little reason to think it would have much influence on co-ordination at the consumption level. Here it is hard to see how anything could be effective short of inter-professional teams with a leader selected, like the Maud Committee's clerk, for his personal qualities rather than his membership of a particular profession.

It is difficult to see such teamwork developing without radical changes in professional education. Charlotte Towle[46] in discussing professional education says 'the problem is that the student may be patterned for inbredness in the long run of his professional life, unless he experiences in these formative years a sense of belonging to a group which highly values its relationship with other groups and which communicates and collaborates effectively with other disciplines in the community'. There is little evidence that current professional education encourages such attitudes. Perhaps common courses in the social sciences, and shared projects during their education would provide a firmer foundation for the future. But the inbredness of today's educators leaves little room for complaisance.

Chapter 8
The balance of power and the consumer

In earlier chapters there have been two constantly recurring themes, the questions of who makes decisions and by what criteria. These questions have been treated as interdependent in the sense that the determination of who takes decisions to some extent determines the criteria by which the decisions are taken. This happens in two ways. First, people have great difficulty in ensuring that they are not influenced in their decisions by personal advantage even when they are trying to act in an objective or altruistic manner, and they may feel under no obligation to make such an attempt. Second, people are limited in their frames of reference by the extent of their knowledge and ignorance as well as by the values they have absorbed in the process of socialisation. This does not mean that a positivist or deterministic view is taken of human behaviour.[1] It is assumed that decisions can be made by people and these can be influenced by rational argument and by appeal to accepted values. Nevertheless, taking into account the real limitations of human judgment whether as expert, or as consumer, or as controller of resources, there is a need to establish a balance of power that ensures that no view is unduly neglected. So far little attention has been given to the question of consumer influence, which is the subject of this final chapter. It is raised in the context of a more general model of factors affecting the balance of power in the provision of social services.

A model of service provision

Donnison[2] in his studies of change in the social services constructed a model which though designed for a different purpose, makes possible an examination of certain factors which influence the balance of power in their provision. Donnison identified three major processes in the provision of a social services : the provision of financial resources; the provision of the service itself; and the consumption of the service. These processes in turn can be further subdivided. The provision of financial resources involves paying the money required through subscriptions, taxes and so on, and also the control of the money which may be separated in the hands of representatives or other intermediaries who regulate demand and expenditure. In the provision of the service one can distinguish between general functions of management, the service itself, and supporting services such as clerical work and domestic service. The consumption of the service includes the processes of referral and selection, as well as direct use.

These different processes can be shared between the participants in a variety of different ways. One of the simplest situations is that of the professional worker in private practice, where almost all the processes, or at least their control, may be divided between the practitioner on the one hand and his clients on the other. The clients consume the product and provide the resources; the practitioner is his own manager and controls supportive services as well as providing all his service. Only referral is likely to remain outside the control of either. In contrast in a large local authority department the processes would be divided between national taxpayers and local ratepayers, the central government executive and local councillors, a variety of specialists within the department and in other departments, referring agents and the consumers themselves.

Any particular group will increase its own power and influence by gaining control over as many of the processes of provision as possible. This is the principle of segmentation. Those it cannot control, it may aim to split between as many groups as possible—the principle of spreading risks. For example, the fundamental weakness of workers in secondary services like paramedical workers in hospitals or welfare officers in education who are providing support for another profession, lies in their lack of control of almost all the relevant processes. Studies have shown how medical social workers in hospitals find that access to resources for expansion, referral of cases and even decisions about the termination of cases are in the hands of others. Moreover they are to a large extent concentrated in the hands of a single group, the medical staff.[3]

In provision through private practice, with almost all the processes divided between the two major participants, there is ostensibly a balance of power between the professional and the consumer, who controls resource provision as well as consumption. This is certainly the basic assumption of those who advocate provision through the economic market when they stress the importance of consumer choice. But in practice the position of most consumers is limited by their ignorance of the criteria by which to judge the quality of the service provided. They are often also in a very vulnerable position, like children in schools or patients made anxious by symptoms they cannot assess.

In state social services the processes are divided between many groups, initially threatening the position of both professionals and consumers. But, as the previous chapter has shown, professionals with their power and authority and their key position in the communication system between consumers and resource providers, have shown a remarkable capacity to reassert their position. Thus the redistribution of power as a result of providing the services through the state appears to be largely at the expense of the consumer. To right the balance consumers need to develop an influence on those who control financial resources equivalent to that of the providers of resources and the providers of services.

Motivations for service provision

If the 'welfare state' could be regarded as a mutual-benefit association on a large scale, as Marshall[4] has suggested, the consumer's position might be better protected. The connection between consumption and the control over resource provision would be reinstated. However, most people do not consider the social services in this light. This is clear from attitudes to the legitimacy of benefits, the stigma attached to many beneficiaries, and the continued acceptance of certain rationing procedures. Basically of course, the public view is right. The essence of mutuality in social-service provision is contingency distribution between people facing similar risks and making similar contributions. But when services are broadened to cover the whole population risks are clearly not the same for everybody. In so far as many contingencies are positively correlated with poverty those who have the lowest risks are likely to contribute most. In so far as services are consciously redistributive of income, they deny the mutuality of benefits.

Traditional mutuality, as a form of insurance, is based on the pragmatic precept 'I will help because this may happen to me or to those I care about'. If the social services, as they now are, are to be seen as 'mutual', then the level of identification must be broadened to include an element of altruism—'I will help because I might have been like this.' This is the basis of philanthropy. It is also essentially the basis of Runciman's concept of social justice,[5] under which the allocation of resources must be acceptable to a reasonable man 'in a state of primordial equality', that is before he knows what his own position in life will be. This requires a considerable effort of imagination.

As Pinker[6] has pointed out Runciman's own research showed how far this concept of social justice was from the attitude of most people, who are limited by their own frame of reference. First, they tend to accept almost wholly the basic ideology of the capitalist market economy. Second, where comparisons are made they generally involve only a few groups whose situation is relatively close to that of the respondent.

In practice the establishment of social services has also been dependent on appeal to two further social precepts. First is the pragmatic 'if we do not help we will suffer', which might be called social protection and betterment. Second, there is the altruistic 'we will help because the society of which we are a part has contributed to the condition of these people', leading to a form of social compensation.

These four motives for social-service provision can be placed in a matrix as in Table 1. Perhaps 'paternalism' should also be added as an additional motive under pragmatic individualism. All these motives have contributed to the development of 'the welfare state', although each of the first three can lead to much narrower approaches—personal insurance, a concern limited to specific groups and a coercive suppression respectively. In

143

TABLE I *Motives for social-service provision*

	Pragmatic	Altruistic
Individual	1 Mutual insurance	2 Philanthropy
Social	3 Social protection and betterment	4 Social compensation

general the social motivations require a broader understanding than the individual, and altruism requires more imagination than pragmatism. This will affect where support can be found for different measures and how the appeal should be made.

The weakness of consumers

Before considering the reasons for the weakness of consumers and how it might be overcome, it is important first to recognise the strength of their position. This lies in their ability to appeal to the motivations which have led to the setting-up of the social services. The latter are not transitory phenomena, and the motives that have led to their being set up represent deep aspirations in the minds of those who have supported them. So it is possible for consumers to appeal to the logic of the situation, to ask a society that wills the ends also to will the means, and to examine the effectiveness of the means currently in use. In doing this, the greatest allies of consumers may often be the professionals and others who work in the social services. It is true that the interests of these two groups do not coincide wholly. There are conflicts of interest such as have been discussed in the previous chapter. But those who work in the services are dependent on consumers in many ways. Consumers justify their salaries. They provide the opportunity to practise skills. They give work satisfaction by responding to treatment and by gratitude or respect. So important indeed are consumers in service provision that Parsons treats them as a form of resource, the regulation of which can be used by society to control service organisations.[7] Consumers have been largely unable to use these sources of power because they have had difficulty in challenging the claim of the 'experts' in the services to define need and to define it in their own terms.

The inability of consumers of social services to exert their full potential influence seems to spring from three factors. They are divided; they have a low status in the services; and they lack knowledge and skills. These factors will be dealt with in order.

While almost all citizens contribute to the cost of services, and therefore have a common interest in economy, over other issues their interests are likely to conflict. The consumers of most services are minorities in society as a whole. For example even parents with dependent children are a minority in the adult population of this country as Margaret Wynn has pointed out.[8] Parents of children with specific handicaps will be an even smaller minority. Many of those in greatest need are the scapegoats of society against whom even others in similar need may unite. So the particularity of individual need and the nature of its incidence tends to isolate consumers from one another.

In recent years there has been a considerable growth of consumer groups with specific needs, such as associations of people with specific handicaps. These groups meet several needs, giving social support and practical advice, raising money for specific objectives as well as exerting political pressure. Frequently in their membership they include some professionals from the services with an interest in the specific condition. Many groups have also arisen whose common interests are based on geographical contiguity—tenants' associations and community councils. A few associations have also been created to represent wider interests such as the Hospital Patients Association, but these often have a smaller membership than associations that bring together those whose more limited concerns but deep anxieties make possible a more whole-hearted and focused commitment. The value of such consumer groups has increasingly been recognised by professionals within the services and by government, and active stimulation has been widely advocated. A new occupational group, community workers, has now grown up specifically to meet this need.

Consumers of the social services also generally have a low status within them. Where the services are provided through hierarchical organisations as they generally are, consumers are the lowest level in the hierarchy. They are often also in a very dependent position because of the compelling nature of their needs or because of the social support for the discipline to which they are subjected. The fear of gaining a reputation as a trouble-maker is very real. This low status within the services is often reinforced by low social status in other spheres. As Pinker[9] has suggested, many of the clients of the social services may be conditioned to the acceptance of a poor service by their experience of the economic market. Perhaps the provision of social services through the economic market was only satisfactory at all because most of those who could pay for services were of an equal or superior social status to the professionals, and so had the authority of status as well as the power of money to back their position. So one of the most important arguments in favour of universal services is that they cover those with high social status as well as those with low, so that the influence of all consumers over the services is likely to be more effective.

Third, consumers of the social services generally lack the knowledge and skills necessary for the evaluation of the services or even to find out what services are provided. The services are complex and organised in a way that makes access difficult for many people. The issues on which consumers need to influence decisions are also complex and technical so that only the well-informed can even ask the right questions, let alone evaluate the answers. Moreover it is in the interests of those who are responsible for the services to make political issues on which lay opinions are relevant appear to be technical issues.[10] This simplifies their task by eliminating criteria that complicate the decisions or are outside their own competence to evaluate. They can thus act decisively and therefore from some points of view more effectively.

Both low status and ignorance can be counteracted by the support and assistance of advisers and advocates. Much advice and some advocacy is provided by workers in the social services employed mainly for other purposes. Social workers particularly have begun to see advocacy as an important part of their role.[11] Officials have been appointed specifically to investigate complaints, like the Parliamentary Commissioner or ombudsman;[12] councils have been set up to represent consumers like the consumer councils of the nationalised industries. Councillors and MPs see advocacy as part of their role. It is a function of consumer associations and of other pressure groups.

A study of consumer consultative machinery in the nationalised industries identified three features of particular significance for effective intervention on the consumer's behalf.[13] The first was the extent to which such bodies were representative of cross-sections of relevant and informed consumer opinion. The second was the extent to which the bodies were organised at levels which corresponded to those of the decision-making bodies with which they were most directly concerned. The third was the right of the bodies to pursue the consumer's case to higher levels of authority, when response had failed at their own level. This may take place within the existing administrative machinery, or a parallel system of adjudication may be set up through the courts or through administrative tribunals.

These three features are of general importance in the development of consumer influence. The first perhaps presents the greatest problems, not so much where individual complaints are being pursued, but where issues are at stake that affect a number of consumers whose needs and interests may vary. It is a matter of first establishing contact, which is difficult, and then maintaining communication in both directions as the situation develops, which is even more difficult. A central problem is that of continuing to negotiate with the relevant decision-making bodies, which involves seeing their point of view, without being subtly converted to neglect of the views of those whose interests are being represented. Fulfilment of the second criterion, the creation of different levels of representation, intensifies the problems by creating additional barriers to communication between negotiators at the top and consumers at the bottom.

Concluding comment

It is generally recognised that social administration, because of its concern with solving human problems, must be concerned with values. Given the two central issues of the distribution of resources, and the distribution of power and authority, Runciman's concept of social justice appears to provide a fruitful basis for reaching agreement on principles.[14] Starting from the position that the principles of allocation must be determined from the point of view of a reasonable man who does not yet know what his own station in life will be, Runciman examines the allocation of income and status.

With regard to the allocation of income, Runciman suggests that it is unlikely that arbiters in such a position would come down in favour of complete equality. For example, special merit and the contribution of the individual to the well-being of the community might be regarded as deserving of reward, while great weight would probably be given to each person's social needs and responsibilities. Although it is impossible to forecast the actual weight that would be given to different criteria, it is certain that the distribution of income would be different from the present distribution, with little room for inherited wealth, and much greater emphasis on need. Runciman however adds a caveat that because social justice demands change, this is not necessarily sufficient justification for trying to effect it, for the process of effecting the change may be too damaging to all those involved to be worth while.

On the question of status Runciman concludes that a distinction would have to be made between respect and praise. He believes that agreement could be reached among rational men that all should be treated with equal respect, but praise would be related to merit. This of course does not accord with the current situation in our society. Here respect is regarded as being due from subordinates to superordinates but not necessarily the other way round. At the same time withdrawal of respect is used as a method of social control. Consumers of the social services suffer from both forms of disrespect. The second leads to the social stigma attached to receiving certain services, and both contribute to the weakness of consumers in obtaining services.

When it comes to the distribution of power and authority the principles that emerge are much less clear cut. First of all, if the principles of social justice applied to the distribution of resources resulted in greater equality of wealth and income, this would in itself reduce inequalities of power between citizens in their private capacities. Second, social justice would also require that those who held power over others must be accountable to others for the exercise of that power. This suggests that power other than the economic power held by citizens in their private capacity would be in the hands either of organs of state or of bodies accountable primarily to those whose situation they controlled—especially employees and consumers. Third, such accountability itself would require a much greater openness in the decision-making processes than occurs today.

It is difficult to see how Runciman's reasoning can be used to take one beyond such safeguards in the use of power. Perhaps the significance of power lies less in the way it is distributed than in the way it is used, and what it achieves. The maximisation of functional autonomy, which is the negation of power, is not in itself more or less desirable than the maximisation of potential through organised joint endeavour, in which hierarchy must have its place. Paternalism need not be incompatible with mutual respect if it is based on true differences in capacity for decision-making and genuine understanding, as it may be in the family situation from which the term is derived. It may be easier to protect the weak in a paternalistic society than in a pluralistic society that apparently gives greater recognition to the reality of conflicting interests.

In effect Runciman's arguments suggest that an ideal distribution of status and of real resources, in so far as they are used for consumption, can be determined irrespective of the reality of human nature or one's view of it. This is not true of the distribution of power. If a person who believes that power always corrupts or that without external control most people will always tend to act irresponsibly, he will advocate quite a different distribution of power from someone who believes differently. In fact the response of people to the possession of power and authority and to subjection to it varies from individual to individual and from culture to culture. So principles would be difficult to enunciate even if those who tried to do so could be objective in their evaluation, and certainly we have no basis in our current knowledge for such objectivity.

But arguments over the distribution of resources and the distribution of power overlap because control over resources is a source of power. It is therefore around issues of power that many differences of principle about the distribution of resources emerge. What proportion of the resources available to society should be used to control behaviour through the provision of incentives? What proportion should be entrusted to individuals in personal income as against the proportion spent on their behalf by the state on the advice of experts?

Finally the power structure of society and of its social services must take into account the technological requirements of the tasks to which it dedicates its endeavours as well as its view of human nature. A strong hierarchical structure seems to be required for some tasks if certain standards of speed, quality, economy or uniformity are to be achieved. Other tasks require a high level of delegation. Either the power structure must be adapted to the requirements or the requirements to the desired power structure.

Notes

Chapter 1   Welfare capitalism and the social services

1   M. Penelope Hall, *Social Services of Modern England*, 2nd ed., Routledge & Kegan Paul, 1953, p. 303.
2   Kathleen M. Slack, *Social Administration and the Citizen*, Michael Joseph, 1966, ch. 4.
3   Mark Abrams, quoted by Slack in ibid., fn. 73.
4   Piet Thoënes, *The Elite in the Welfare State*, ed. J. Banks, Faber & Faber, 1966, p. 125.
5   T. H. Marshall, 'Value problems of Welfare-Capitalism', *Journal of Social Policy*, vol. 1, pt 1, January 1972. Marshall attributes the term 'Welfare-Capitalism' to Crossman in R. H. Crossman (ed.), *New Fabian Essays*, Turnstile, 1952, pp. 6 and 25.
6   Max Weber, *The Protestant Ethic and the Spirit of Capitalism*, trans. T. Parsons, Allen & Unwin, 1952 : R. W. Green (ed.), *Protestantism and Capitalism: the Weber Thesis and its Critics*, Heath, 1959.
7   Adam Smith himself was far more willing to qualify his theoretical propositions than some of his successors, but of even more relevance to behaviour was the popularisation of these theories in a particularly simplified form. For example consider the following quotation from a character in Mrs Gaskell's *North and South*. 'if [the book] told you what he said it did, that wages find their own level, and that the most successful strike can only force them up for a moment, to sink in far greater proportion afterwards, in consequence of that very strike, the book would have told you the truth.' (Everyman ed., 1963, p. 221). Mrs Gaskell was a very humane writer, concerned about the wrongs suffered by workers, and anxious to humanise the relationships between masters and men, but the context of the quotation shows that she herself would have accepted this view.
    This contrasts with Adam Smith's recognition that the level of wages is affected by the weakness of the workers in rela-

tion to their masters, who 'are always and everywhere in a sort of tacit, but constant and uniform, combination not to raise the wages of labour above their actual rate'. (*The Wealth of Nations*, book 1, ch. 6).

8   Ibid., book 1.

9   See the discussion in Robert A. Dahl and Charles E. Lindblom, *Politics, Economics, and Welfare*, Harper & Row, 1953. All references are to the Torchbook edition of 1963. See pp. 68–78 and 173.

10 Paul A. Samuelson, *Economics: an Introductory Analysis*, 6th ed., McGraw-Hill, 1964, p. 37.

11 On the whole the conventional economic approach tends to be very uncritical of the market economy as a distributive and co-ordinative system. See e.g. Samuelson, op. cit., pp. 450–2 and 611–17. Dahl and Lindblom give a more critical approach in a different framework on the lines followed here; op. cit., pp. 385–93.

12 B. Seebohm Rowntree, *Poverty: a Study of Town Life*, Macmillan, 1901, p. 87.

13 See the discussion of Keynesian Theory in any economics text-book, e.g. Samuelson, op. cit., ch. 11.

14 For the importance of marginal theory to economics follow the references in the index of any text-book. See the comments of Dahl and Lindblom, op. cit., p. 408.

15 E.g. Samuelson, op. cit., pp. 753–4.

16 J. K. Galbraith, *The New Industrial State*, Hamish Hamilton, 1967.

17 G. H. Peters, *Cost-Benefit Analysis and Public Expenditure*, Eaton Paper no. 8, Institute of Economic Affairs, 1966.

18 See p. 83 below.

19 The conventional economic view is described by Samuelson, op. cit., pp. 609–17, and is further elucidated in Abram Bergson, *Essays in Normative Economics*, Harvard University Press, 1966, esp. chs 1 and 3. For a critical approach which I have generally followed, see Maurice Dobb, *Welfare Economics and the Economics of Socialism: towards a Common Sense Critique*, Cambridge University Press, 1969.

20 Bergson, op. cit., p. 15 and ch. 3.

21 Ibid., pp. 52ff; M. Dobb, op. cit., pp. 213–14.

22 Dahl and Lindblom, op. cit., p. 391.

23 Alfred Marshall, *Principles of Economics*, 9th ed., Cambridge University Press, 1961, pp. 119–23.

24 T. H. Marshall, op. cit.

25 The philosophy of the Institute of Economic Affairs is summed up in the paper by several of its members, *Towards a Welfare Society*, IEA, 1967.
26 R. M. Titmuss, *Commitment to Welfare*, Allen & Unwin, 1968. For a discussion of the issues see R. Pinker, *Social Theory and Social Policy*, Heinemann Educational, 1971, ch. 3. For a summary of the arguments see Anthony Forder (ed.), *Penelope Hall's Social Services of England and Wales*, 2nd ed., Routledge & Kegan Paul, 1971, pp. 334–8.
27 Hall, op. cit., 6th ed., Routledge & Kegan Paul, 1963, pp. 3–4 (repeated from earlier editions).
28 Peter M. Blau and W. Richard Scott, *Formal Organizations*, Routledge & Kegan Paul, 1963.
29 Gilbert Smith, *Social Work and the Sociology of Organisations*, Routledge & Kegan Paul, 1970.

Chapter 2 Resources, income and wealth

1 The income received from land is called 'rent' by economists and its tendency to rise or fall independently of the efforts of the rentier is discussed in all economic text-books. A similar phenomenon is the income of those with special skills that cannot be produced to order in response to increased demand, known as 'quasi-rent'.
2 M. Young and P. Willmott, *Family and Kinship in East London*, Routledge & Kegan Paul, 1957.
3 *Report of the Expert Committee on Compensation and Betterment* (Uthwatt Report), Cmd 6383, HMSO, 1942.
4 Harry Street, *Justice in the Welfare State*, Stevens, 1968, ch. 4, 'Licensing'.
5 Ministry of Land and Natural Resources, and Scottish Department, *The Land Commission*, Cmnd 2771, HMSO, 1965.
6 Alfred Marshall, *Principles of Economics*, 9th ed., Cambridge University Press, 1961, pp. 762–4.
7 The recognition of this was an important influence in the 'human relations' school of management, described in most text-books on organsations and management, e.g. A. Etzioni (ed.), *Modern Organisations*, Prentice Hall, 1964.
8 T. S. Simey, *The Concept of Love in Child Care*, National Children's Home, 1960.
9 Rosemary Stevens, *Medical Practice in Modern England—the Impact of Specialisation and State Medicine*, Yale University Press, 1966, pp. 242–6 and 146. The Willink Report in 1957

actually recommended a 10 per cent reduction in the enrolment of medical students because of fear of producing too many doctors although by the following year it was clear that this was quite mistaken.

10 G. S. Shackle, *Economics for Pleasure*, Cambridge University Press, 1959.

11 For a fuller exposition of these issues see N. Kaldor, *An Expenditure Tax*, Allen & Unwin, 1955; *Final Report of the Royal Commission on Taxation*, Cmd 9474, HMSO, 1955; Memorandum of dissent by Mr G. Woodcock, Mr H. L. Bullock and Mr N. Kaldor, pp. 354ff; Richard M. Titmuss, *Income Distribution and Social Change*, Allen & Unwin, 1962, ch. 2.

12 The main sources for this section are Jack Revell, *The Wealth of the Nation: the National Balance Sheet of the United Kingdom, 1957–61*, Cambridge University Press, 1967: Central Statistical Office, 1956, *National Income Statistics—Sources and Methods*, 1956. See also *Annual Abstract of Statistics*, and *Social Trends*, for up to date information.

13 See the discussion of the effect of this on forward estimates of government expenditure in *Public Expenditure 1968–69 and 1973–74*, HMSO, 1969, paras 77–8.

14 Ministry of Housing and Local Government, *Our Older Homes: a Call for Action* (Dennington Report), HMSO, 1968.

15 Brian Abel-Smith, 'Public expenditure on the social services', *Social Trends*, no. 1, 1970.

16 Wynne Godley and Christopher Taylor, 'Public sector's rising claim on resources', and 'Heavier tax burden and reduced consumption', *The Times*, 17 and 22 February 1971.

17 Titmuss, op. cit., provides the main source for this discussion.

18 Department of Employment (prev. Ministry of Labour) *Family Expenditure Survey*. See also Ministry of Agriculture, Fisheries and Food, *Household Food Consumption and Expenditure* (annual).

19 Child Poverty Action Group (CPAG), *The Cohabitation Rule: a Guide for Single, Separated, Divorced or Widowed Women claiming Supplementary Benefit or National Insurance*, Poverty Leaflet no. 4, January 1972.

20 First introduced under the Magistrates' Courts (Matrimonial Proceedings) Act 1958.

21 See discussion and references in Anthony Forder (ed.), *Penelope Hall's Social Services of England and Wales*, 2nd ed., Routledge & Kegan Paul, 1971, pp. 119–20.

22 For example take two individuals who become liable to income tax at 30 per cent for income over £25 per week, and also both have an income that averages exactly this figure. The income of the first is irregular and in a four-week period he receives £20 for two weeks and £30 for two weeks. The second receives £25 each week. If tax is calculated on a weekly time unit, the first will pay £3 tax, the second no tax. If the tax unit is a month, neither will pay tax.

23 Ministry of Social Security, *The Circumstances of Families*, HMSO, 1968, para. 22.

24 Published regularly in the *Employment and Productivity Gazette*.

25 Barbara Wootton, *The Social Foundations of Wages Policy*, 2nd ed., Allen & Unwin, 1962.

26 E.g. N. Bosanquet and R. J. Stephens, 'Another look at low pay', *Journal of Social Policy*, vol. 1, pt 3, July 1972. National Board for Prices and Incomes, *General Problems of Low Pay*, Cmnd 4648, HMSO, 1971.

27 *Family Expenditure Survey*.

28 Titmuss, op. cit.

29 See *Social Trends* for annual comment on the figures. For a discussion of the method of collection see Revell, op. cit. and Titmuss, op. cit.

30 See Molly Meacher, *Rate Rebates—a Study of the Effectiveness of Means-Tests*, CPAG, 1973.

31 Ministry of Social Security, *Annual Report 1966*, Cmnd 3338, HMSO, 1967, pp. 60-1.

32 P. R. Kaim-Caudle, 'Selectivity and the social services', *Lloyds Bank Review*, 1969; A. R. Prest, *Social Benefits and Tax Rates*, IEA, 1970.

33 Jean Cresswell and Pauline Parker, 'The frail who lead the frail', *New Society*, vol. 20, 25 May 1972, pp. 407-10.

34 Ministry of Pensions and National Insurance, HMSO, 1966.

35 Dennis Marsden, *Mothers Alone: Poverty and the Fatherless Family*, Allen Lane, 1969.

36 See Forder, op. cit., pp. 103 and 116 for a comment on developments to 1968. Since then until the date of writing (April 1973) there have been no further increases.

37 Ann Cartwright provides some evidence that GPs who consider that patients bring too many trivial complaints to them successfully reduce the number of consultations. Old people also have a reluctance to approach GPs with many complaints

though this is only partly due to reluctance to trouble GPs. Ann Cartwright, *Patients and their Doctors*, Routledge & Kegan Paul, 1967, pp. 44–6 and 195–204. It is difficult to find evidence of attitudes to private practice.

38 Sheila Kay, 'Problems of accepting means-tested benefits' in David Bull (ed.), *Family Poverty*, Duckworth, 1971, pp. 30–1. Virginia Bottomley, in a small study of fourteen families, says 'throughout the whole group ran the belief that to apply for these [means-tested] benefits was a form of begging', *Families with Low Income in London*, CPAG, 1971.

39 See n. 35.

40 I know of no systematic evidence of this but draw on personal experience in social work and elsewhere for these comments.

41 For an example of the effect of fear of dependence see Burns's comment on the household means test and family break-up noted in ch. 4, n. 9.

42 R. Pinker, *Social Theory and Social Policy*, Heinemann Educational, 1971.

Chapter 3 The definition of need

1 R. Walton, 'Need: a central concept', *Social Service Review*, July 1969.

2 Kathleen M. Slack, *Social Administration and the Citizen*, Michael Joseph, 1966, chs 6 and 7.

3 Office of Health Economics, *Malnutrition in the 1960's*, 1967.

4 *The Times*, 15 January 1970.

5 From the Constitution of the World Health Organisation (WHO) (1947) quoted in K. Soddy (ed.), *Cross Cultural Studies in Mental Health*, Tavistock, 1961, p. 70.

6 Russell Barton, *Institutional Neurosis*, John Wright, 1959.

7 Soddy, op. cit., pt II, 'Mental health and value systems'. K. Soddy and Robert E. Ahrenfeldt, *Mental Health and Contemporary Thought*, Tavistock and Lippincott, 1967, pt II, 'Problems of conceptualisation'.

8 J. Bowlby, *Maternal Care and Mental Health*, WHO, 1951. It may be worth noting that just as the concept of health is developed as the antithesis of definable ill-health, so Bowlby's hypothesis came from a study of maternal deprivation which was particularly apposite in the aftermath of the war.

9 Barbara Wootton, *Social Science and Social Pathology*, Allen & Unwin, 1959, ch. 10, and 'A social scientist's approach to

material deprivation', in WHO, *Deprivation of Maternal Care —A Reassessment of its Effects*, 1962.

10 Margaret Mead, 'A cultural anthropologist's approach to maternal deprivation', in ibid.

11 R. D. King, N. V. Raynes and J. Tizard, *Patterns of Residential Care: Sociological Studies in Institutions for Handicapped Children*, Routledge & Kegan Paul, 1970.

12 B. Seebohm Rowntree, *Poverty: a Study of Town Life*, Macmillan, 1901, ch. 4.

13 Ibid., p. 87.

14 Ibid., p. 97.

15 Ibid., pp. 107-8.

16 Ibid., p. 99.

17 B. Seebohm Rowntree, *Poverty and Progress: a Second Social Survey of York*, Longman, Green, 1941.

18 P. Townsend, 'Measuring poverty', *British Journal of Sociology*, June 1954.

19 Minimum building standards were established through local by-laws under the Public Health Act 1875 and later legislation. Rowntree, op. cit., uses the standard of overcrowding of the Registrar-General.

20 Ministry of Housing and Local Government, Welsh Office, *Old Houses into New Homes*, Cmnd 3602, HMSO, 1968, Appendix. The fifth basic amenity for which improvement grants are available is a ventilated food store.

21 Ministry of Housing and Local Government, Central Housing Advisory Committee, *Homes for Today and Tomorrow*, HMSO, 1961.

22 Ministry of Housing and Local Government, *The Housing Programme 1965 to 1970*, HMSO, 1965.

23 *The Revised Code 1862*, quoted in J. Stuart Maclure (ed.), *Educational Documents: England and Wales 1816 to 1967*, Methuen, 1965, pp. 79-80.

24 The recognition of this is, for instance, implied in the conclusion that grades of secondary education (ending at the ages of 14, 16 and 18 or 19) 'correspond roughly, but by no means exactly, to the gradations of society' (Maclure, op. cit., pp. 92ff).

25 DES, Central Advisory Council for Education (England), *Children and their Primary Schools*, HMSO, 1967, para. 151.

26 Spastics Society and National Association of Mental Health, *A Right to Love?*, 1972.

27 Social Science Research Council, *Research on Poverty*, Heinemann, 1968, p. 5.
28 W. G. Runciman, *Relative Deprivation and Social Justice*, Routledge & Kegan Paul, 1966.
29 H. H. Gerth and C. Wright Mills (eds), *From Max Weber: Essays in Sociology*, Kegan Paul, Trench, Trubner, 1947, pp. 181ff.
30 Morton S. Baratz and William G. Grigsby, 'Thoughts on poverty and its elimination', *Journal of Social Policy*, vol. 1, pt 2, April 1972.
31 The terms 'welfare values' and 'deference values' are attributed by Baratz and Grigsby to Harold D. Lasswell and Abraham Kaplan, *Power and Society*, Yale University Press, 1950.
32 Walton, op. cit.
33 Ronald Lippett *et al.*, *The Dynamics of Planned Change*, Harcourt, Brace & World, 1958, p. 66.
34 Runciman, op. cit.
35 Ken Coates and Richard Silburn, *St Ann's: Poverty, Deprivation and Morale*, Nottingham University, Department of Adult Education, 1967.
36 R. W. Halsall and W. H. Lloyd, 'Admission of elderly people to hospital', *British Medical Journal*, 30 December 1961.
37 K. Roberts, 'The entry into employment: an approach towards a general theory', *Sociological Review*, vol. 16, 1968, pp. 165–84.
38 Lippett *et al.*, op. cit., pp. 65–8.
39 On the failure of psychiatric treatment for autism see Hale F. Shirley, *Pediatric Psychiatry*, Harvard University Press, 1963, p. 612. On hospital care of the mentally subnormal see Pauline Morris, *Put Away: a Sociological Study of Institutions for the Mentally Retarded*, Routledge & Kegan Paul, 1969.
40 King, Raynes and Tizard, op. cit.
41 Victor George and Paul Wilding, 'Social values, social class and social policy', *Social and Economic Administration*, vol. 6, no. 3, September 1972.
42 Ibid.

Chapter 4   The distribution of resources

1 W. G. Runciman, 'Social justice', *Listener*, 29 July 1965, reprinted in Eric Butterworth and David Weir, *The Sociology of Modern Man*, Fontana/Collins, 1970, p. 308. See also W. G.

Runciman, *Relative Deprivation and Social Justice*, Routledge & Kegan Paul, 1966.

2 Barbara Wootton, *The Social Foundations of Wages Policy*, 2nd ed., Allen & Unwin, 1962.

3 Guy Routh, *Occupation and Pay in Great Britain, 1906–1960*, Cambridge University Press, 1965, p. 147.

4 *Occupational Pension Schemes, 1971—Fourth Survey by the Government Actuary*, HMSO, 1972.

5 P. Holman (ed.), *Socially Deprived Families in Britain*, National Council of Social Service, London, 1970.

6 Ministry of Social Security, *Circumstances of Families*, HMSO, 1967, Tables II. 3, II. 6, VI. 8, and VI. 9.

7 E. M. Burns, *British Unemployment Programs, 1920–38*, Washington Committee on Social Security, 1941, esp. pp. 160–6.

8 Jean Cresswell and Pauline Parker, 'The frail who lead the frail', *New Society*, vol. 20, 20 May 1972, pp. 407–10.

9 Such family break-ups did occur though they were less common than was believed at the time. The dependent relative was as likely to leave as the 'liable relative', but sanctions could be employed on the latter. Burns, op. cit., p. 247.

10 The official view is more optimistic than that of some commentators. Office of Manpower Economics, *Equal Pay: First Report on the Implementation of the Equal Pay Act, 1970*, HMSO, 1969.

11 Peter Moss, *Welfare Rights Project '68*, Merseyside Child Poverty Action Group, 1969; Sheila Kay, 'Problems of accepting means-tested benefits', in David Bull (ed.), *Family Poverty*, Duckworth, 1971, pp. 30–1.

12 E.g. Molly Meacher, *Rate Rebates—a Study of the Effectiveness of Means-Tests*, CPAG, 1973, pp. 26–7.

13 B. Seebohm Rowntree, *Poverty: a Study of Town Life*, Macmillan, 1901.

14 *Social Insurance and Allied Services; a Report by Sir William Beveridge*, Cmd 6402, HMSO, 1942, para. 347.

15 R. M. Titmuss, *Commitment to Welfare*, Allen & Unwin, 1968, p. 179.

16 Department of Health and Social Security, *National Superannuation and Social Insurance: Proposals for Earnings-Related Social Security*, Cmnd 3883, HMSO, 1969. There is no statement of how the surplus would be used, unlike the original proposals in 1957. For comment see Tony Lynes, *Labour's Pension Plan*, Fabian Tract 396, 1969, p. 10, where

arguments about the relative methods of 'funded' and 'pay-as-you-go' schemes are also marshalled.

17 John Vaizey, *The Costs of Education*, Allen & Unwin, 1958, pp. 23, 84, 101–2. Note the obscure wording on p. 84 corrected in the summary on p. 23.

18 Adrian L. Webb and Jack E. B. Sieve, *Income Redistribution and the Welfare State*, Occasional Papers in Social Administration no. 41, G. Bell, 1971, pp. 11–12 and p. 14, fn. 4.

19 Ibid., p. 13.

20 E.g. Brian Abel-Smith, *Labour's Social Plans*, Fabian Tract 369, 1966, ch. 5, 'Why not raise taxation?'

21 E.g. Titmuss, op. cit., p. 122.

22 Burns, writing of the inter-war period said, 'The most common argument in favour of a means test of whatever type is the assertion that, in the words of the Royal Commission of 1930–32, "While the resources available are as limited as they are today, we should think it unfortunate if payments were made to persons who were not in need, at the expense ultimately of those who are most in need" '. Op. cit., p. 240, quoting *Unemployment Insurance*, Report of the Royal Commission, 1932.

23 E.g. Titmuss, op. cit., ch. 16, 'The role of redistribution in social policy'.

24 Martin Rein, 'Social class and the health service', *New Society*, 20 November 1969.

25 Published in *Economic Trends* in various issues from 1962 onwards. See also J. H. Nicholson, *Redistribution of Income in the United Kingdom in 1959, 1957 and 1953*, Bowes & Bowes, 1965.

26 Webb and Sieve, op. cit.; A. Peacock and R. Shannon, 'The welfare state and the redistribution of income', *Westminster Bank Review*, August 1968.

27 Webb and Sieve, op. cit., ch. 7.

28 Bleddyn Davies, *Social Needs and Resources in Local Services*, Michael Joseph, 1968, p. 16.

29 Bleddyn Davies, 'Welfare departments and territorial justice', *Social and Economic Administration*, October 1969.

30 Rosemary Stevens, *Medical Practice in Modern England—the Impact of Specialisation and State Medicine*, Yale University Press, 1966, Table 20, p. 225.

31 King Edward's Hospital Fund for London, 1964, Dr Shaw, *Report on Communications and Relationships between General Practitioners and Hospital Medical Staff*.

32 See the introduction to Ministry of Health, *A Hospital Plan for England and Wales*, Cmnd 1604, HMSO, 1962. This plan, of course, represents an attempt to correct the disparities—an attempt which is largely absent in the approach to local authority services.

33 Bleddyn Davies, *Variations in Services for the Aged: a Causal Analysis*, Occasional Papers in Social Administration no. 40, G. Bell, 1971.

34 Noel Boaden, *Urban Policy-Making: Influences on County Boroughs in England and Wales*, Cambridge University Press, 1971.

35 D. N. Chester, *Central and Local Government: Financial and Administrative Relations*, Macmillan, 1951, ch. 10.

36 Davies, *Variations in Services for the Aged*.

37 Boaden, op. cit.

38 Chester, op. cit., pp. 303ff.

39 M. Flynn, P. Flynn, and N. Mellor, 'Social malaise research: a study in Liverpool', *Social Trends*, no. 3, 1972.

40 Davies, *Social Needs and Resources in Local Services*, chs 8, 11 and 12.

41 On educational priority areas see DES, A. H. Halsey, *Educational Priorities*, 1972. On the Home Office projects, see John Banks, 'The role of central government', in Anne Lapping (ed.), *Community Action*, Fabian Tract 400, 1970. On Urban Aid see Teresa and George Smith, 'Urban first aid', *New Society*, vol. 19, 30 December 1971, pp. 1277–80.

42 Department of Economic Affairs, *The Intermediate Areas*, Cmnd 3998, HMSO, 1968.

43 Stephen Hatch and Roger Sherrott, 'Positive discrimination and the distribution of deprivations', *Policy and Politics*, vol. 1, no. 3, March 1973.

44 J. A. G. Griffith, *Central Departments and Local Authorities*, Allen & Unwin, 1966, pp. 88ff.

45 Ibid., pp. 90–1.

46 Ibid., chs 2 and 4 (esp. p. 290).

47 Described in Edward Blishen (ed.), *Blond's Encyclopedia of Education*, Blond Educational, 1969, p. 592.

48 Stevens, op. cit., pp. 223ff.

49 Home Office and Scottish Department, *Report of the Departmental Committee on the Probation Service* (Morison Report), Cmnd 1650, HMSO, 1962, para. 195.

50 R. A. Parker, 'Social administration and scarcity', *Social Work* (London), April 1967.

51 G. H. Peters, *Cost-Benefit Analysis and Public Expenditure*, Eaton Paper no. 8, IEA, 1966.

52 Peter Self, 'Nonsense on stilts: the futility of Roskill', *New Society*, vol. 16, no. 405, 2 July 1970, pp. 8–11. Peter Hall, 'The Roskill argument: an analysis', *New Society*, vol. 17, no. 435, 28 January 1971, pp. 145–9 and Peter Self's letter in reply p. 206.

53 See references in Peters, op. cit.

54 Mark Blaug, 'The rate of return on investment in education in Great Britain', *Manchester School of Economic and Social Studies*, vol. 33, no. 3, September 1965; 'The economic return on investment in higher education in England and Wales', *Economic Trends*, May 1971; S. J. Mushkin, 'Health as investment', *Journal of Political Economy*, vol. 70 (supplement), October 1962.

55 But see the criticisms in the Report of the Robbins Committee, chaired by an economist, *Higher Education*, Cmnd 2154, HMSO, 1963, paras 620–30.

56 For an account of cost-analysis methods, and illustrative references, see John G. Hill, 'Cost analysis of social work service', in Norman A. Polansky, *Social Work Research*, Chicago University Press, 1960. For comment on the difference between measuring effect and effectiveness, see the following paper in this work by Martin Wolins.

57 Anthony Forder, T. Reti and J. R. Silver, 'Communication in the Health Service: a case study of the rehabilitation of paraplegic patients', *Social and Economic Administration*, vol. 3, no. 1, January 1969. See pp. 88–90.

Chapter 5   Co-ordination

1 Kathleen M. Slack, *Social Administration and the Citizen*, Michael Joseph, 1966, ch. 11, 'Avoidance of conflict'.

2 Basil Bernstein, 'Social class and linguistic development: a theory of social learning', in A. H. Halsey, J. Floud and C. A. Anderson (eds), *Education, Economy and Society*, Free Press, 1958.

3 Jean Nursten, 'Social work, social class and speech systems', *Social Work* (London), vol. 22, no. 4.

4 Anthony Forder, T. Reti and J. R. Silver, 'Communication in the Health Service: a case study of the rehabilitation of paraplegic patients', *Social and Economic Administration*, vol. 3, no. 1, January 1969.

5   Peter M. Blau and W. Richard Scott, *Formal Organizations: a Comparative Approach*, Routledge & Kegan Paul, 1963, ch. 5.
6   R. W. Revans, 'Hospital attitudes and communications', in *Sociology and Medicine*, Sociological Review Monograph no. 5; and *Standards for Morale*, Oxford University Press, 1964.
7   Blau and Scott, op. cit., pp. 124–8.
8   Olive Stevenson, 'Co-ordination reviewed', *Case Conference*, vol. 9, no. 8, February 1963.
9   Ibid.
10 Peter Boss, 'Child care and the development of a family service', pp. 269–70 in Anthony Forder (ed.), *Penelope Hall's Social Services of England and Wales*, 2nd ed., Routledge & Kegan Paul, 1971. John Greve, Dilys Page and Stella Greve, *Homelessness in London*, Scottish Academic Press, 1971, esp. chs 6–9.
11 Cyril A. Hagan, William Blair and Norman J. Smith, 'Adults with special needs', pp. 298–300. In Forder (ed.), op. cit.
12 See e.g. G. F. Rehin and F. M. Martin, 'Psychiatric services in 1975', *Political and Economic Planning*, vol. 29, no. 468, 1963. *Towards Community Care*, Political and Economic Planning, 1969.
13 For example see R. Wager, *Care of the Elderly: an Exercise in Cost Benefit Analysis Commissioned by Essex County Council*, Institute of Municipal Treasurers and Accountants, 1972.
14 Barbara N. Rodgers *et al.*, *Comparative Social Administration*, Allen & Unwin, 1968, pt II, ch. 3.
15 A rather awkward but useful phrase coined by Lippett and his colleagues to cover both individual clients and the situation where a complex system such as an organisation or community is receiving a service R. Lippett *et al.*, *The Dynamics of Planned Change*, Harcourt, Brace & World, 1958.

Chapter 6   Power, authority and freedom

1   Max Weber, *The Theory of Social and Economic Organisation*, A. M. Henderson and Talcott Parsons (trans. and ed.), Free Press and Falcon's Wing Press, 1947, p. 324; quoted in Peter M. Blau and W. Richard Scott, *Formal Organizations: a Comparative Approach*, Routledge & Kegan Paul, 1963, p. 28. See also H. H. Gerth and C. Wright Mills (eds), *From Max Weber: Essays in Sociology*, Kegan Paul, Trench, Trubner, 1947, p. 180.

2 Weber, op. cit., quoted in Blau and Scott, op. cit.
3 Amitai Etzioni, *The Active Society*, Free Press, 1961, p. 360.
4 Joyce Warham, *An Introduction to Administration for Social Workers*, Routledge & Kegan Paul, 1967, p. 52. Harvey and Mills suggest a typology of power based on the two dimensions of legitimacy and sanctions:

Legitimacy of Power

		High	Low
Ability to	High	Legal authority	Coercion
impose sanctions	Low	Rational authority (expertise)	Persuasion manipulation

Edward Harvey and Russell Mills, 'Patterns of organisational adaptation' in Mayer N. Zald (ed.), *Power in Organisations*, Vanderbilt University Press, 1970, p. 203.
5 Gerth and Mills, op. cit., p. 180.
6 Amitai Etzioni, *A Comparative Analysis of Complex Organisations*, Routledge & Kegan Paul, 1970, pp. 14ff.
7 Michael Crozier, *The Bureaucratic Phenomenon*, Tavistock, 1964.
8 Gerth and Mills, op. cit., pp. 295–9. See also Max Weber, 'The three types of legitimate rule', trans. Hans Gerth in A. Etzioni, *A Sociological Reader in Complex Organisations*, 2nd ed., Holt, Rinehart & Winston, 1969.
9 Warham, op. cit., p. 52.
10 Paul M. Harrison, *Authority and Power in the Free Church Tradition*, Princeton University Press, 1959. Harrison's concept of rational-pragmatic authority includes 'professional authority', but the latter is too ill-defined a concept to be useful. See the comments on professionalism in the next chapter.
11 For a vivid analysis of decision-making in a psychiatric hospital that illustrates the pluralism of its structure see A. Strauss, L. Schatzman, D. Erlich and R. Bucker, 'The hospital and its negotiated order' in E. Friedson (ed.), *The Hospital in Modern Society*, Macmillan, 1963, reprinted in F. G. Castles, D. J. Murray, and D. C. Potter, *Decisions, Organisations and Society*, Penguin, 1971.
12 The concept of the front-line worker has particular significance in Smith's analysis of 'front-line organisations'. Dorothy

Smith, 'Front line organisation of the state mental hospital', *Administrative Science Quarterly*, vol. 10, 1965, pp. 381–99; discussed in Gilbert Smith, *Social Work and the Sociology of Organizations*, Routledge & Kegan Paul, 1970.

13 Alvin W. Gouldner, 'Reciprocity and autonomy in functional theory', in L. Gross (ed.), *Symposium on Sociological Theory*, Harper & Row, 1959.

14 pp. 5–7.

15 *Higher Education* (Robbins Report), Cmnd 2154, HMSO, 1963, paras 340–3. See also ch. 14, 'Academic freedom and its scope'.

16 H. S. Ferns, *Towards an Independent University*, IEA, 1969, esp. pp. 16–18. In the four years since these proposals were put forward, the planning of the independent university has proceeded to the extent of appointing a Vice-Chancellor.

17 Ralph M. Kramer, 'Ideology, status and power in board executive relationships', *Social Work* (New York), vol. 10, no. 4, October 1965. Anthony Forder, 'Lay committees and professional workers in the English probation service', *Social and Economic Administration*, vol. 3, no. 4, October 1969.

18 D. V. Donnison, Valerie Chapman *et al.*, *Social Policy and Administration: Studies in the Development of Social Services at the Local Level*, Allen & Unwin, 1965, chs 10 and 11.

19 E.g. F. H. Hayek, 'The road to serfdom', in A. V. S. Lockhead (ed.), *A Reader in Social Administration*, Constable, 1968. But see also R. M. Titmuss, *The Irresponsible Society*, Fabian Tract 323, 1960.

20 *Occupational Pension Schemes 1971—Fourth Survey by the Government Actuary*, HMSO, 1972, pp. 47–50.

21 E.g. under the contracting out arrangements for graduated pensions under the National Insurance Act 1959.

22 Under the Redundancy Payments Act 1965.

23 National Council of Social Service, *Citizens' Advice Notes*, 1973, (14) 30.

24 Barbara N. Rodgers *et al.*, *Comparative Social Administration*, Allen & Unwin, 1968, ch. 2.

25 See the defence of current arrangements in *Report of the Charity Commissioners for England and Wales for the Year 1969*, HMSO, 1970, paras 7–16, and the comment in *New Society*, vol. 20, p. 628.

26 The low proportion of subsidy for many voluntary organisations was shown in a study of voluntary organisations in

Liverpool by students for the Liverpool University Diploma in Social Administration 1967–8. Report available from the Department of Sociology.

27 A. D. Lindsay, 'Conclusion', pp. 305–6 in A. F. C. Bourdillon (ed.), *Voluntary Social Services: their Place in the Modern State*, Methuen, 1945.

28 T. H. Marshall, *Sociology at the Crossroads*, Heinemann, 1963, ch. 16, pp. 339–41.

29 A. F. Philp, *Family Failure*, Faber & Faber, 1963.

30 Gordon Matthews, 'Philosophy, methods and aims of the Simon Community', *Case Conference*, January 1969. Neither this article nor the Philp's book in the previous note claims that the work done by voluntary organisations could not be undertaken by the state.

31 Established under the Race Relations Act 1965.

32 Arthur Willcocks, *The Creation of the National Health Service*, Routledge & Kegan Paul, 1967; Michael Ryan, 'The tripartite administration of the National Health Service—its genesis and reform', *Social and Economic Administration*, September 1972.

33 DES, *Education and Science in 1967*, Cmnd 3564, HMSO, 1967, para. 133.

34 Olive Keidan, 'The health services' in Anthony Forder (ed.), *Penelope Hall's Social Services of England and Wales*, 2nd ed., Routledge & Kegan Paul, 1971, pp. 182–3.

35 Forder, 'Lay committees and professional workers in the English probation service'.

36 J. A. G. Griffith, *Central Departments and Local Authorities*, Allen & Unwin, for the Royal Institute of Public Administration 1966, esp. pp. 17–18 and 505ff.

37 Noel Boaden, *Urban Policy-Making—Influences on County Boroughs in England and Wales*, Cambridge University Press, 1971. Ch. 1 gives an account of approaches to this issue and of the lack of evidence about it.

38 Griffith, op. cit.

39 Ibid., pp. 515ff.

40 pp. 44–8.

41 Boaden, op. cit.

42 Michael B. Gaine, 'Education', in Forder (ed.), *Penelope Hall's Social Services in England and Wales*, pp. 55–6.

43 Housing Finance Act 1972.

44 Local Government (Financial Provisions) Act 1963, section 6.

45 Rodgers *et al.*, op. cit., pp. 27–8.

46 *Social Insurance and Allied Services; a Report by Sir William Beveridge*, Cmd 6402, HMSO, 1942, para. 44.

47 Ibid., paras 44–7, 161–5.

48 Ibid., para. 163.

49 D. N. Chester, *Central and Local Government: Financial and Administrative Relations*, Macmillan, 1951, ch. 5.

Chapter 7 Professionalism and the structure of the social services

1 Ernest Greenwood, 'Attributes of a profession', *Social Work* (New York), vol. 2, no. 3, July 1957. Republished in Howard M. Vollmer and Donald L. Mills (eds), *Professionalisation*, Prentice Hall, 1966.

2 A. Etzioni (ed.), *The Semi-Professions*, Free Press, 1969.

3 C. Turner and M. N. Hodge, 'Occupations and professions', in J. A. Jackson (ed.), *Professions and Professionalisation*, Cambridge University Press, Sociological Studies 3, 1970.

4 A. M. Carr-Saunders and P. A. Wilson, *The Professions*, Oxford University Press, 1933, pp. 294–5. See also T. H. Marshall, *Sociology at the Crossroads*, Heinemann, 1963, p. 153.

5 H. Jamous and B. Peloille, 'Professions or self-perpetuating systems? Changes in the French university-hospital system', in Jackson, op. cit.

6 Theodore Caplow, *The Sociology of Work*, University of Minnesota Press, 1954, reprinted in Vollmer and Mills, op. cit., pp. 20–1.

7 G. Harries-Jenkins, 'Professionals in organisations, in Jackson, op. cit.

8 Harries-Jenkins, op. cit.

9 Caplow, op. cit.

10 Bentley B. Gilbert, *The Evolution of National Insurance in Great Britain*, Michael Joseph, 1966, pp. 303–10.

11 Peter M. Blau and W. Richard Scott, *Formal Organisations: a Comparative Approach*, Routledge & Kegan Paul, London, 1963, pp. 60–3. Blau and Scott are comparing 'professionalism' and 'bureaucratic organisation', and it is not always clear whether they are concerned with the norms governing individual or collective practice. This leads to a difficulty in considering the question of whether decisions are based on self-interest. As the authors say, the decisions of some formal organisations are expected to be based on self-interest which contrasts with the position of the professional practitioner who

167

is expected to subordinate self-interest to the needs of the client. On the other hand the bureaucrat, as opposed to his organisation, is like the professional in having to subordinate self-interest to other criteria but in his case to the goals of the organisation.

12 Mark Abrahamson, *The Professional in the Organisation*, Rand McNally, 1967, ch. 4 and pp. 126–7.

13 Burton R. Clark, 'Faculty organisation and authority', in T. F. Lunsford, *The Study of Academic Administration*, Western Interstate Commission for Higher Education, 1963; reprinted in Vollmer and Mills, op. cit.

14 For an example of the results of an extreme centralisation in the allocation of residential vacancies in response to a situation of shortage, see David Donnison, Valerie Chapman *et al.*, *Social Policy and Administration: Studies in the Social Services at the Local Level*, Allen & Unwin, 1965, pp. 99ff.

15 Rosemary Stevens, *Medical Practice in Modern England—the Impact of Specialisation and State Medicine*, Yale University Press, 1966, pp. 146–7.

16 Ministry of Health, *Final Report of the Committee on Costs of Prescribing* (Hinchcliffe), HMSO, 1959, esp. ch. 2 : Almont Lindsey, *Socialised Medicine in England and Wales: the National Health Service 1948–1961*, Oxford University Press, 1962, pp. 200–1.

17 See ch. 5.

18 Lucille N. Austin, 'An evaluation of supervision', *Social Casework*, vol. 57, no. 8, 1956. Other references are listed in Donald A. Devis, 'Teaching and administrative functions in supervision', *Social Work* (New York), vol. 10, no. 2, April 1965.

19 Alvin W. Gouldner, 'Reciprocity and autonomy in functional theory', in L. Gross (ed.), *Symposium on Sociological Theory*, Harper & Row, 1959.

20 Philip E. Hammond and Robert E. Mitchell, 'Segmentation of radicalism—the case of the protestant campus ministers', *American Journal of Sociology*, 71, 1965, abridged and reprinted in Abrahamson, op. cit.

21 Marjorie Moon and Kathleen M. Slack, *The First Two Years: a Study of the Work Experience of some Newly Qualified Medical Social Workers*, Institute of Medical Social Workers, c. 1964. Zofia Butrym, *Medical Social Work in Action*, G. Bell, 1968.

22 Hence the strength of opinion among social workers against

the appointment of medical officers to positions as directors of social services. This is occasionally reflected in the social-work journals, e.g. *Social Work Today*, vol. 1, no. 8, p. 18; vol. 2, no. 5, p. 26.

23   Anne Corbett, 'No more kid-catchers', *New Society*, vol. 17, 4 March 1971, pp. 352–3.

24   Dan C. Lortie, 'The balance of control and autonomy in elementary school teaching', in Etzioni, op. cit., esp. pp. 30–41.

25   Anthony Forder, 'Lay committees and professional workers in the English probation service', *Social and Economic Administration*, vol. 3, no. 4, October 1969.

26   Stevens, op. cit., pp. 310–19. General practitioners have still managed to retain their independence under the reorganisation of the National Health Service in 1974.

27   This may be primarily a weakness in professional educational curricula or there may be deeper psychological factors, arising from the importance of skills in the self-image of the individual.

28   Ministry of Housing and Local Government, *Report of the Committee on the Management of Local Government*, HMSO, 1967, vol. 1, paras 103–8.

29   See n. 15.

30   *Higher Education* (Robbins Report), Cmnd 2154, HMSO, 1963, paras 257 and 264, and Appendix 3, Table 14.

31   See ch. 6, p. 100 and n. 7.

32   Bernard Barber, 'Some problems in the sociology of professions', *Daedalus*, 92 (Fall, 1963), abridged and reprinted in Abrahamson, op. cit.

33   Gilbert, op. cit., chs 6 and 7, esp. pp. 362–8, 401–2, 429–37. Arthur Willcocks shows how in the creation of the National Health Service practitioners relied on the same strategies to protect their freedom—*The Creation of the National Health Service*, Routledge & Kegan Paul, 1967.

34   Ch. 6, nn. 15 and 16.

35   Forder, op. cit.

36   Home Office, *Report of the Care of Children Committee*, Cmd 6922, HMSO, 1946. See also Jean Heywood, *Children in Care*, 2nd ed., Routledge & Kegan Paul, 1965, chs 8 and 9.

37   See Donnison, Chapman *et al.*, op. cit., ch. 8; Gladys M. Kammerer, *British and American Child Welfare Services*, Wayne State University Press, 1962.

38   In 1956 of 1,031 child care officers, 25 per cent had a professional qualification and 41 per cent a social-science qualifi-

cation (Younghusband Report, Table 30). Ten years later the figures were 2,693, 32 per cent and 21 per cent respectively (Seebohm Report, Appendix M, pt II).

39 Home Office, *Report of the Committee on Children and Young Persons* (Ingleby Report), Cmnd 1191, HMSO, 1960; Scottish Department, *Report of the Committee on Children and Young Persons (Scotland)* (Kilbrandon Report), Cmnd 2603, HMSO, 1964; Labour Party, 1964, *Crime—A Challenge to Us All* (Longford Report).

40 Home Office, DES, Ministry of Housing and Ministry of Health, *Report of the Committee on Local Authority and Allied Personal Social Services*, Cmnd 3703, HMSO, 1968.

41 Department of Health and Social Security, HMSO, 1970, para. 31.

42 See ch. 5.

43 E.g. Ministry of Health, *Management Functions of Hospital Doctors*, HMSO, 1966; Department of Health and Social Security, *Management Arrangements for the Reorganised National Health Service*, HMSO, 1972; *The Civil Service*, Cmnd 3638, HMSO, 1968, vol. 1, ch. 5 and vol. 2.

44 Ministry of Housing and Local Government, *Report of the Committee on the Management of Local Government*.

45 Ibid., para. 152.

46 Charlotte Towle, *The Learner in Education for the Professions as seen in Education for Social Work*, University of Chicago Press, 1954, p. 49.

Chapter 8   *The balance of power and the consumer*

1 See the discussion of these issues in Victor George and Paul Wilding, 'Social values, social class and social policy', *Social and Economic Administration*, vol. 6, no. 3, September 1972.

2 D. V. Donnison, Valerie Chapman *et al.*, *Social Policy and Administration: Studies in the Development of Social Services at the Local Level*, Allen & Unwin, 1965, pp. 231–6.

3 Marjorie Moon and Kathleen M. Slack, *The First Two Years: a Study of the Work Experience of Some Newly Qualified Medical Social Workers*, Institute of Medical Social Workers, c. 1964: Zofia T. Butrym, *Medical Social Work in Action*, G. Bell, 1968.

4 T. H. Marshall, *Sociology at the Crossroads*, Heinemann, 1963, p. 331.

5 W. G. Runciman, *Relative Deprivation and Social Justice*, Routledge & Kegan Paul, 1966, pp. 252ff.

6 R. Pinker, *Social Theory and Social Policy*, Heinemann Educational, 1971, pp. 113–15.

7 Talcott Parsons, *Structure and Process in Modern Societies*, Free Press, 1960, chs 1 and 2.

8 Margaret Wynn, *Family Policy*, Michael Joseph, 1970, pp. 23–5.

9 Pinker, op. cit., pp. 142–3.

10 Piet Thoënes, *The Elite in the Welfare State*, ed. J. Banks, Faber & Faber, 1966, pt II.

11 E.g. The Ad Hoc Committee on Advocacy, 'The social worker as advocate: champion of social victims', in R. W. Klenk and R. M. Ryan (eds), *The Practice of Social Work*, Wadsworth, 1970.

12 Annual reports of the Parliamentary Commissioner, HMSO; Harry Street, *Justice in the Welfare State*, Stevens, 1968, ch. 5.

13 Consumer Council, *Consumer Consultative Machinery in the Nationalised Industries*, 1968, ch. 6.

14 Runciman, op. cit.

Index of authors

Government papers are not listed except for reports known by the name of the chairman, e.g. Beveridge Report.

Index of subjects

In some cases the reference is to the general subject of a passage even though the specific word does not appear in the text. Particularly detailed treatment is given to the key concepts dealt with in the book.